THE BRONTËS OF BALLYNASKEAGH

Cottage in Emdale—Patrick's Birthplace—St. Patrick's Day 1777.

THE BRONTËS OF
BALLYNASKEAGH

By
W. Haughton Crowe

1978
DUNDALGAN PRESS (W. TEMPEST) LTD.
DUNDALK

To Rosemary and Vincent

ISBN 0-85221-100-7

© W. Haughton Crowe

PREFACE

This is a story based on the life of Hugh Brontë, grandfather of the Haworth family. It is not history in the more rigid sense, but much of it is Hugh's own story which we may or may not accept at its face value. For the most part I have drawn on the account given by Dr. Wright in his *Brontës in Ireland*, adding a little here and there from *Wuthering Heights*, and from *Man of Sorrow* by John Locke and W. T. Dixon, and from letters published in the *Banbridge Chronicle*.

Such is the backcloth; the rest is, I hope, reasonable speculation on what may have happened. Whether or not the incidents took place exactly as recorded is irrelevant; the salient points are that Hugh Brontë's boyhood was remarkable; that his love live with Alice (or Eleanor) deserves to be remembered as one of our great rural love stories; and that through his son Patrick he had an indirect influence on the creation of two of the world's most famous novels: *Jane Eyre* and *Wuthering Heights*.

Rostrevor, 1978

LIST OF ILLUSTRATIONS

CONTENTS

ACKNOWLEDGMENT

I wish to acknowledge with gratitude my indebtedness to Mr. Maurice Ferguson, A.R.I.B.A. for allowing me to use his fine drawings of many of the places mentioned in the book.

CHAPTER 1

BY THE BANKS OF THE
BOYNE WATER

A T a time when the countryside bordering on the banks of the River Boyne had scarcely recovered from the blood-bath between the forces of William of Orange and James the First of England, a long low farmhouse stood slightly up a hillside overlooking the river with its flagon-flanked meadows and scrubby swamps. If you could look out from the windows of this house, which you couldn't as it has long since disappeared, and if you had periscopic eyes you would see a graceful wide stream meandering this way and that between heavily wooded hills, and under the now beautiful village of Slane with its sacred hill, where Patrick lit the paschal fires; and, looking further, you might be able to see away on up to Laracor where Swift lived and loved his Stella.

All this and more you might see in this blood-soaked Boyne-soaked, and legend-soaked land. Here it was that artist and artisan, poet and peasant, philosopher, statesman and saint had lived and outlived their days. From those honey-filled fields to the north Malachy of Mellifont began his fateful journey to Rome: a journey that was to end in an unending friendship with Bernard of Clairvaux. And it was in the lands to the south of Newgrange that Eithne—or Boand, who gave her name to the Boyne, lived—or at least so the legend says—with her husband Eleman. It was at Newgrange, too, that the ancient art of the Irish first began to appear in those beautiful abstract intertwinings and interlacings that were

I

ultimately to flower in later days into the exquisite patterns
of Celtic art.

Many centuries later a poet, F. R. Higgins, was to write:

> Only last week, walking the hushed fields
> Of our most lovely Meath, now thinned by
>   November,
> I came to where the road from Laracor leads
> To the Boyne river—that seemed more lake
>   than river,
> Stretched in uneasy light and stript of reeds.
>
> And walking longside an old weir
> Of my people's, where nothing stirs—only
>   the shadowed
> Leaden flight of a heron up the lean air !
> I went unmanly with grief, knowing how my
>   father,
> Happy though captive in years, walked with
>   me there.

How much do we owe to our fathers, grandfathers, great-
grandfathers, and all those who walked before us ? How much
do we owe to the land on which they walked and the soil on
which they were nurtured ? In what subtle ways were the
genes in the innermost recesses of our cellular bodies influenced
by the brown earth of our being ? It may well be that some
biologists know the answers to these questions; but I doubt it.
Such questions may forever remain unanswerable.

And yet it seems a reasonable assumption that, since the air
we breathe, the water we drink, and the earth that grows the
substances necessary for our well-being, influence our bodies,
then these must also influence our minds, and to some extent
the bodies and minds of those who come after us.   Some
writers maintain that every story begins with Adam. The
logic of such a thesis is irrefutable, but so far—or so far as I
know—only in one book has any attempt been made to do this.
For the rest of us humbler and less-inspired wielders of the

pen the best we can do is to hark back to parents, grand-parents, and occasionally to great-grandparents, or even great-great-grandparents.

Our story begins with the great-great-grandparents and the great-grandparents of the family Brontë, Bronty, Brunty, Prunty. Of the various spellings and pronunciations you may take your choice, for neither spelling, nor pronunciation were very important when few people could either read or write, and in a country where pronunciations could change accord-ing to the accent of the pronouncer. Though the ë may have been substituted later, we shall, for the purposes of this story, and to avoid confusion, use the Brontë spelling.

At the outset then the great-great-grandparents on the Brontë side were to be found with their roots deep in the rich loam alongside the Boyne water. It would be all too easy to draw the—probably erroneous—conclusion that, because they had their roots in this most fertile, and most civilized part of Ireland, they were ultimately to produce, as their descendants, one of the most outstanding literary families in all Britain. It might also be equally erroneous to conclude that, because some of these roots were to be uplifted and transplanted to an equally beautiful and fertile part of the County Down, this also contributed to the ultimate flowering of genius. Whatever our conclusion the fact remains that all this was to happen.

The former tenant of this long, low, thatched farm-house on the banks of the Boyne was none other than a certain Hugh Brontë. He was a big man with crisp, dark hair, and blue eyes which gleamed in a way that showed both intelligence and kindliness. And his house, reflecting the personality of its owner, also gleamed with golden thatch and limewash. Entering the house you would find yourself in the open turf-fire-warmed kitchen, with its crane-suspended pots and pans, its plain, scrubbed dresser, and its equally plain table and chairs borne precariously on the uneven flagged floor. A narrow passage in front of the kitchen jamb-wall may have given access to a room where guests would have been entertained, while it is likely there were partitioned bed-rooms at the other end. The man or girl would have slept in warmth, if not in comfort, in a ladder approached loft over the kitchen. Outside hens, pigs, and ducks probably cackled, grunted and quacked in the cobbled yard beyond the half-door.

Behind the shelter of wind-breaking trees cows and horses were doubtless penned in ill-conditioned, ill-lit byres and stables, beyond which a mucky midden would have been a happy hunting ground for ducks, and a children's nightmare. Rakes, and hay-rakes, wheels, and wheelbarrows, and all other items and implements used in traditional methods of farming, were to be found lying around here and there with little regard for organization, and less for work and motion study.

Our man was a farmer in a country where cropping com-manded less attention than grazing the lush meadow lands; and, being above average in intelligence, shrewdness, and the gift of speech, he soon found that there were more rapid and more profitable ways of turning a penny—honest or other-wise—than in tilling the earth, however fertile. Thus he discovered that short-term grazing could bring long-term profits, both in an immediate financial sense, and also in a steady build up of the resources of his soil. In other words he was a believer in the dictum: 'never sell anything from your land that cannot walk off on four legs'; and he might have added that between sales it is better to give your land a good airing.

But like all other peasant farmers enough farming was done to supply the house. There were always a few cows in milk, or strippers with little milk, but large in-calf bellies; and each evening and morning the unhygienic milk could be heard hissing into pails. Without milk there would be no butter, and without butter no buttermilk, both necessary for the survival of man and beast. And of course there was the inevit-able potato, the mainstay of Irish life and living when the crop was good, and the destroyer of life and living in the bad years.

Spuds and butter, milk and buttermilk, bacon and eggs, and maybe fruit of sorts from a brambly, nettle-choked untended orchard; these were always at hand—all good food, and all that was necessary for the maintenance of healthy life.

And health was necessary; for the life that Hugh Brontë—great-great-grandfather Brontë—had chosen was far from easy. It was, in fact, a hard, tough life, not only because of its contacts with tough men, but also, as everyone with any knowledge of cattle knows, the management of stampeding beasts in all weathers demands a strong constitution, a heart of iron, and lungs like a pair of blacksmith's bellows. In those days, too, travelling on board a cattle ship from Drogheda to Liverpool was not everybody's idea of a pleasure cruise.

So it was with mixed feelings that Mrs. Brontë heard her husband say on one fateful evening in early summer when a batch of cattle, looking glossy and well-conditioned from their feed of early grass, were to be delivered for sale in the markets across the Irish Sea:

" Listen, me darlin'," he said as he stroked one of his dogs stretched out in the heat of the kitchen fire, " get yer best hat and clothes together; for if the weather holds it's off to Liverpool we'll be in the mornin'."

" Och ! " said she, " can ye not go be yerself for once ? Sure I'd only be a burden to ye; and besides there's far too much to be looked after here. There's the hens, and the chicks, an' who's goin' to give the calves their sup when I'm not here ? "

" Ah, come on now," Hugh said, for he loved his wife and never felt happy without her. " Sure if Ah went away me lone, it's only the half of meself would be with me. An' that's a right man and girl we have now; the two o' them and the children'll look after things."

" Ah, well," sighed Mrs. Brontë with an air of resignation, " since ye put it that way Ah suppose Ah'll have to be goin' with ye; but ye can have the right ould sootherin' tongue when ye want me to do somethin' for ye. Have ye made any arrangements ? Do ye know what time the boat's due to sail ?

Have ye the cattle ready; an' have ye talked it over with the others ? An' ye know we have to have food for the journey, an' there are your clothes an' mine. Yer a typical man ! Ye'd think there was nothin' to do but pack up and go ! Ye see about as far ahead o' ye as a blind man in a fog."

" Time enough ! time enough ! " said Hugh, as he knocked out the dottle of his pipe on the hearthstone. " Plenty o' time, plenty o' time in the mornin'. The boat'll not sail before evenin' anyhow."

The following morning Hugh was up as soon as the sun shot its first tentative rays over the Irish Sea. Scarcely had the dewdrops begun to glint in the meadows, and the Boyne water to turn to silver in streams and shallows, than a great bustling and shouting could be heard around the house. What a din there was ! Bellowing beasts, barking dogs, and the thwacks of sticks on tough hides, and men calling all the imprecations of hell on animals whose illegitimacy they proclaimed in no uncertain terms.

Soon, however, steers, stores, and fat heifers were gathered together in one struggling, sweating mass, and the lot were on their way down river to the Drogheda docks where the ship with furled sails was well berthed. And now, added to the shouts and curses of cattlemen were those of the sailors, until at last all the frightened reluctant animals were safely installed in their dank, dark holds where, foodless and waterless, and on the insubstantial ground of a rolling ship, they had to remain for many hours to come.

In the meantime at the house Hugh and his lady and their small cabin trunk were up on the family conveyance; Hugh in the driving seat with the reins between his hands looking smart, handsome, and in high spirits, and his lady in flounces and frills feeling like a girl about to set out on her honeymoon. A few last instructions to the family and servants; and, with a crack of the whip, they were off on a journey as fateful for them as it was for the world of English literature.

CHAPTER 2

LIVERPOOL LEAVE-TAKING

HAVING disposed of the cattle the Brontë pair, with good money in their pockets, were compelled to stay in Liverpool lodgings for a night or two before making the return journey. The weather had broken with a portentous and violent thunderstorm; there was no question of departure until this had subsided. Even when eventually the captain decided to set sail the skies, lit by flashes of sheet lightning, were ominous and lowering, and the ship rolled heavily in the ground-swell aftermath of the storm. Before the storm broke, however, Mrs. Brontë, with typical feminine thought for those at home, had purchased hats and hosiery, dolls and balls for the youngsters, tobacco for himself and trinkets for the older ones. Little did she realize that before many hours had passed she would be bringing home a different type of present in her already overladen arms.

Scarcely were they aboard on that dark and threatening evening when above the cries of

" Heave away, there ! "

" Up the mainsail ! "

" Hard a-port ! "

and all the other cries, calls, creaks and crankings associated with the departure of a ship under sail, there was heard an unusual noise: the whimpering cry of an infant; it appeared to come from the hold.

There was pandemonium when it was discovered that the cries came from a dirty, dark, little brat tied in a bundle and left in the hold with some other parcels.

7

" What the hell's going on down there ? " shouted the captain.

" Haul away there, haul away, or we'll not be in Ireland afore Christmas ! "

" Ah, toss the brat overboard ! " somebody said, " sure he'll only bring us bad luck; an' mebbe be the death o' the lot of us ! "

But Mrs. Brontë, a strong, forceful, and kindly woman, would have none of it. Her maternal heart was stirred to its depths. Furiously thrusting her way forward through the motley crowd on deck, she lifted the unsavoury child in her arms; and facing the rest of them with blazing eyes she shouted:

" Ah, ye dirty pack o' villains, would ye be afther murdher-ing one o' God's own creatures ? What sort o' hearts have ye at all, at all ? "

Taken aback, and feeling guilty, the unsympathetic crowd drew aside and allowed the good lady to have her way, while she, for her part, made soothing sounds to the infant; at the same time she used her own clean kerchief in an effort to remove some of the filth and grime from his dark features. Turning to her husband, who was at her side throughout the incident, she said decisively:

" We'll have to bring him with us, Hugh; there's no other way."

" Och, sure I know," Hugh replied, " but what the hell are we going to do with him when we get him home ? "

" Ah dunno, Hugh; but God would never forgive us if we left him to the mercies of these ruffians. Surely somebody, or some institution, 'll take pity on him. Anyhow we'll look after him throughout the voyage; an' no doubt we'll find an answer at the end of it. Once he's cleaned up the captain might accept responsibility for returning him to some authority in Liverpool."

The good lady soon had the child washed and fed, and safely abed in their small cabin, but she was never to forget the terrible night that was to follow. The storm they thought they had left in Liverpool seemed to break loose with redoubled fury when they were well out in the open sea. Sails were lowered and hatches battened down; and the ship tossed, turned, plunged, and rolled like a bucking horse. Roaring storm and rolling thunder became indistinguishable, and there were times when even Hugh thought their last hour had come. The foundling whimpered, wept and screamed by turns. Mrs. Brontë, feeling queasy and distracted, devotedly wished she had never embarked on such an adventure.

But the terrors of the night are almost worth enduring for the solace of a new day, especially when the day, after a night of storm, dawns fresh and clear. This proved to be the case; the hell of the night before had given place to a glorious heaven of sparkling calm sea; and so when the Brontës went on deck that morning they found the ship steadily heading westwards toward the green shores of Meath and home.

As time went in those days it was not long before they made a landfall; and found themselves sailing majestically between the green and wooded slopes of the Boyne. Soon they came to rest, and with much shouting and orders ropes curled through the air like uncoiling snakes.

" Lower away there ! lower away ! " In a trice gangways were out and they were ashore.

Having found food and clothing for the child in Drogheda they returned to the ship, where Hugh had some words with the captain.

" Look here," said Hugh, " this child's your responsibility; he was found on board your ship, an' ye'll have to take him back an' hand him over to the authorities in Liverpool. Moreover, I'll make enquiries; an' if there's any hanky-panky you'll be held responsible."

But the captain proved to be a hard man; and though Hugh could be tough when the occasion demanded, short of a stand up fight, he could make no progress. Besides, if it came to a quarrel the main sufferer would be the child.

" You took him on," the captain bellowed, " an' ye's can bloody well go ahead with the job now. He's not comin' back on my ship, an' that's that ! "

Kindly woman though she was, Mrs. Brontë had no wish to have another mouth to feed; and indeed she had inward misgivings about bringing this unattractive child into her already large family. But the child, by that strange chemistry which seems to attract unlikely human beings toward each other, appeared to have taken a fancy to Hugh who, like most other farmers at that time, was not averse to what might prove to be a helpful addition to the family.

However, a woman's common sense prevailed, with the result that, before long, and before leaving Drogheda, they had made intensive inquiries about having the infant placed in some kind of care. Their inquiries were fruitless. Hugh knew a lawyer in the town who informed him that there was no suitable institution in Drogheda; that the only possibility was to take the child to Dublin where, on payment of a vestry tax, it might be possible to get him into a foundling hospital. As such an arrangement was, for the time at least, impracticable, the only solution seemed to be to take the boy home. This they did; and great was the excitement when at last they drew rein at the old homestead.

There is always excitement about a homecoming, even in normal circumstances, and especially when there are children around.

" What did you bring us, Papa ? "

" What did you bring us, Mama ? "

These were the questions after the usual family salutations.

" And now," said Mama, after the distribution of the presents: one final bit of excitement ! " and from the well of the car she withdrew the sleeping child.

Of course the girls displayed their interest at once; and as each one pinched, and cooed, and asked a thousand questions, the infant, for the first time and almost the last, showed affection and joy; and actually smiled.

But in spite of the smile, it was not a pleasant looking creature: it was dark-haired, sallow, and foreign-looking, with slightly protruding teeth, and eyes that squinted a little. Altogether it was unprepossessing; and while it, because of its helplessness, aroused a certain maternal instinct in the girls, the boys had no such feelings.

" Where the hell did ye get that brat from ? " said one of the older adolescents, " sure 'tis a gypsy he is."

" There's no need to use language like that," Mama replied, " an' he's no gypsy—Welsh maybe—an' we found him all his lone in the cargo on the boat. Nobody took pity on him except your good Papa and meself; so here he is for better or for worse; he'll have to stay among ye for the time being at least."

Welsh he may have been, but Welsh he was to remain: he was, in fact, to be known by this nickname for the rest of his life. Indeed what began as a nickname became a Christian name which was eventually to become a family name. Though the Brontë boys were no more unkindly than others of their day and age, and age group, none-the-less, like most lads, they had a slight tendency to bully or—to use a colloquialism—" take the Micky out of " those who were younger, weaker, and unable to fit into the general pattern.

" And now," said Mama, " Ah want ye to get the wee bouchaleen ready for his first sup in the house. Papa and me are tired out after the long journey, an' we'd like to get to bed early. For to-night, anyhow, the little one can sleep in the wall-bed in our room."

Before long the family were seated around the well-scrubbed deal table in the flagged kitchen, while the great glowing turf fire added its comforting warmth to the inner warmth of a homecoming and a reunited family. They needed no spirits other than their own high spirits, and no speeches with which to express their feelings. Food there was in plenty: golden-topped fresh baked " cake " from the hearth oven, spuds, butter, eggs, milk, oaten farls, blackberry and apple jelly, and the lot washed down by the over-twelves with great draughts of strong, sweet tea.

Only the mite in the wall bed had caused any misgivings.

Indeed that night as Mr. and Mrs. Brontë lay in their feather-bed under the warm thatch, Hugh said:

" Ah've been wonderin' me love if we've done the right thing. Ah can't see the children—the boys in particular—accepting the wee fella."

" Och," said Mrs. Brontë, " would ye take yer rest now; an' quit worryin'; everything 'll look different in the mornin'. Besides, the boy has certainly taken to you."

" Aye, aye, don't Ah know ! But if that goes on it's not goin' to help, for it'll mebbe make the others jealous."

The conversation would make it appear that in this case, at least, the roles of the man and the woman had been reversed, for it is usual for the woman to worry, and the man to accept life as it comes. But there are many exceptions to the usual, and many circumstances that can change what is generally accepted. Hugh, with a certain prophetic awareness of things to come, counted many more sheep that night than he had ever possessed, before the blessed balm of sleep eventually caused his eyelids to close, and his mind to cease meandering.

In the morning things did look different. And what a day it was ! How good to be home again ! Hugh, always sensitive to his surroundings and, like many of his fellow countrymen, with something of the poet in him, peered through the latticed windows to see the morning mists lifting gently from sweet flag and meadow-sweet, and from the tree-lined valleys of his beloved Boyne-land, while a thousand birds trilled, and chortled, whistled, and sang such a cacophony of sound, the like of which no city-dwelling late-lier would hear in a lifetime. God ! how good it was to be alive !

Already the men were out, dogs were barking, roosters calling the newborn day, and hens announcing proudly the laying of the first eggs. In the byre the gentle mooing of a cow indicated that her time was near, so Hugh's first task was to throw off his jacket to assist the cow when necessary; this was a job he would trust to no one other than himself. Expertly he ran his hand over the flushed udder; then feeling the softened pin-bone just under the tail, he knew that he had timed things almost to the minute. Soon the padding animal began to press; before very long her efforts resulted in the protrusion of two tiny hooves, which Hugh drew on gently outwards and downwards each time the cow pressed. Next came the difficult moments for both cow and man, the expulsion of the head. Once this was accomplished the rest was easy. And behold a new bundle of life was there; a miracle had been performed.

Having attended to this matter, Hugh was soon on horse-back across hill and dale, flat-land, and water meadow to make sure that all his cattle were accounted, comfortable, and healthy. This one might have to be impounded, maybe it had a bit of a cough—all too common where the worms were down beside the river—or another might look dull and blown from too much new grass. These would have to be dosed with the rough and ready traditional cures of those times when veterinary knowledge was not of a very high order.

While all this was going on, Hugh had not given a thought to the events of the last few days; it was only when hunger drove him to the breakfast table that he suddenly remembered about the foundling child. The girls had him washed, dressed, and ready for his breakfast. Until the arrival of the boss his incurious eyes showed little sign of interest in anyone. The usual attempts were made to gain some response: gurgling noises, animal sounds, objects of one sort or another, toys; everything was tried, but without success. The childish face remained unaffectionate and impassive. Indeed if those present could have foreseen all that was to happen in the future, they would have been convinced of the horrifying view that a man's character is patterned in his blood-stream from birth.

It was only when Hugh arrived that the unattractive face and eyes suddenly became transformed with interest and affection. It has been said that men like dogs because dogs, by their faithfulness and love for their masters, flatter their egos. Possibly it was for the same reason that the child's attachment to Hugh—an attachment which was to have fateful and near fatal consequences—found a ready response.

CHAPTER 3

THE BIG DRIVE

" HIE you there ! Pat, James, at the rick ! The rest o' yes follow me wi' the forks and rakes. We've got to get the field cleared by nightfall. Work hard now, the lot o' ye; there's no time to be wasted ! "

" An' what about me ? " said young Welsh. " I'll follow you, master, wi' the rake."

" Right," agreed Hugh, always giving in to the wishes of the youngster, who had already grown out of a childhood which had never been childhood in the generally accepted sense. He had become, like many another apparently delicate child, old-fashioned; and because he was delicate, not only old-fashioned, but spoiled—by Hugh in particular. All this had led to some bullying which, in turn, had produced the usual vicious cycle, bending still further a fundamentally twisted nature.

It had always been the same; when anything good was going he got the lion's share. Special tit-bits would be surreptitiously transferred from Hugh's plate to his. When Hugh had been in town, or away in Liverpool, Welsh's hand would be the first into the man's pocket to find the goodies he had brought home with him. The boy would always be at his heels, looking for the easy and pleasant jobs, avoiding the rough and dirty work. When there was a chance of a tandem ride on horseback, Welsh would be the one to be up behind the master.

Mrs. Brontë, intuitively sensing trouble ahead, often tried to remonstrate with her masterly man.

" Ye know ye must treat him the same as the others, or there'll be jealousy," she would say. " Besides it's not good for any lad to spoil him."

" Sure he's only a wee delicate critter with neither kith nor kin," he would reply. " Ye can't treat him like a normal child. The way ahead is clear for the others: education, work, money, and women, if and when they want them. But what is there for him ? Nothin'—nothin' at all ! "

Mrs. Brontë pondered these things in her heart; but only replied with a woman's sigh of resignation.

As Welsh grew up and the boys grew up, things became worse. Sometimes the boys, having been more than usually incensed by some piece of unfair treatment, would try to get their own back. On the very day when this chapter of our story began, for example, the boys got together and decided to build a hay-rick specially high, so that when they knew Welsh to be on the other side they were able to push the mass of hay on top of him. Hugh, hearing the screams and shouts, was not slow to react:

" Ye young spalpeens," he roared, " if yiz do the like o' that again Ah'll strap yez within an inch o' yer lives ! "

Anger in a normally equable and kindly man is more terrifying than when it occurs with those less well-disposed. Thus it was that Hugh's sons were at once fearful and crest-fallen. But their repentance was to be shortlived, for at the next opportunity they " dunted " the boy through a hedge; and on another occasion they ducked him in the river.

Each event was duly reported to his benefactor; and many other events that never happened; some were grossly exaggerated. It is not unusual for boys at school, when charged with bullying, to say: " But, sir, he asked for it." This is often the case; there is a certain type of boy whose temperament, appearance, manner, and indeed, actions, are such as to ask for it; and the problem with which a master is often faced is the age-old chicken-egg problem. Did the boy, by his actions, incite this sort of thing? Or did the other lads drive a physically weak type into foolish actions? Such questions never appeared to disturb Hugh's mind. His own boys were always in the wrong; finding this to be the case Welsh soon learned how to profit. The result was that Hugh and the boy were to become inseparable; more and more Hugh came to depend on the boy for duties both important and unimportant: anything from helping him to put on his boots in the morning to giving information about how much men expected for cattle at fair or auction. The inevitable happened: as Welsh grew up and became more aware of the ways of men, he came to know too much about the affairs of Mr. Hugh Brontë.

Often the two would go off to a cattle fair near by. While Hugh would be talking to this or that crony, or haggling with another man, Welsh would be off mingling here and there among the drovers and drivers, cattle men and callers, mistresses and wives, and the general motley of men, women and children to be found at every fair, sale, and market throughout the country. The gypsy-like looking lad excited no comment, for gypsies were as common at fairs as flies on a window-pane in summer. Wandering around with incurious eyes and open ears, he might hear something like this:

"How are ye, Pat?"

"Och, not too bad, Joe; an' how's yerself?"

"Och I'm all right; but sure 'tis a cold day."

"A cold day it is, Pat, an' have ye much for sale?"

"Not much indeed, a brace or two o' stores. The times are hard and the grazin's scarce."

"Aye, aye, man, it's hard to make a livin' these days, an' the more ye make the more them landlords are askin' in rent."

"How much do you expect for the stores, Pat?"

"Och, now, man, Ah'd be lucky to get tin a head, or mebbe tin and a half."

Any such conversation would be duly reported back to Hugh who, keeping Welsh in the background, would ask:

" How much for the lot ? "

" Ah'd be losin' money if Ah took fifty," would be the reply.

" Fifty! Och, man, do ye think Ah'm made o' money ? Ah'll give ye forty an' no questions asked."

" All right, then, forty it is; but 'tis a hard man ye are."

" Hard or not, give us yer han' on it," said Hugh, as his hand hit the other's with a whack that could be heard from one end of the fairground to the other.

As the two repaired to the inn to seal the bargain over the best of what the inn had to offer, Welsh, listening, seeing, and listening again, would continue his meanderings among the multitude. He knew there would be a small cut for himself. This he would increase by buying sugary sweetmeats, baubles and bangles, and other trinkets and trumpery, which he would sell to the family, and others, at a profit.

As he became older, too, his shrewd mind, educated in the three R's by whatever local schools and masters were available, began to speculate and calculate on Hugh's worth, so that when the day of reckoning came for all the snubs and insults he had endured, he would know on how much he could reckon.

The girls took little notice of him—with the exception of one, the youngest and prettiest, Mary. On her, in a remote sort of way, he lavished many kindnesses, often giving her the the sweets and baubles he sold to the others. If it is the case that opposites in the two sexes are attracted toward each other, then the idea certainly applied in this case, for no two could have been more opposite in character, temperament, and appearance. Mary was pretty to the extent of being almost beautiful; she was dark-haired, blue-eyed; and though often gay, and generous, she could at times be introverted and quiet. Was she really attracted toward this ugly, swarthy fellow who was so completely alien in character and manner compared with the rest of the family that he was heartily disliked by all of them? Perhaps we shall have an answer to this question as the story unfolds. It may well be, however, that in some strange way, as adolescence merged into womanhood, her physical desires were stimulated by his ruthless character, and unpleasant appearance. For whatever reason some young women are attracted toward a man in whom they recognize characteristics which are the direct opposite of their ideal.

In the meantime, before the final *dénouement*, there were many clashes between the foundling and his foster brothers and sisters; these became more violent as the family grew up. Some of the events concerned no doubt made such a deep impression that they were passed on to succeeding generations, and eventually found their way into the pages of *Wuthering Heights*.

There is little doubt that the other members of the Brontë household were afraid of Welsh. Why? Because the members of any community are always afraid of those who break the rules: the boy who tells the master, the worker who tells the boss; the little matters of life are better settled among the people directly concerned, for little matters can so easily escalate when carried from little people to bigger ones.

The incident of the two colts has been told with variations by different members of the family. It appears that Hugh, having returned from a successful cattle sale, had given one of the boys, and Welsh, enough money with which to buy horses for themselves. Hugh considered it would be good training for the youths to purchase their own mounts, even should it mean making their own mistakes. Accordingly, the son went to a local fair, and Welsh to one further afield.

On returning Welsh discovered that he had made a mistake: his horse proved to be lame. As the two were dismounting at the stables, the surly Welsh, mad that somebody had done better than him, and that he would look a fool, couldn't contain himself; he came up behind the son as he was about to hang up his saddle, and knocked him off his feet. But he had taken on more than he had bargained for; a fight followed in which Welsh was badly bruised and knocked about. Cornered at last he shouted:

"If ye don't give me your bloody horse, Ah'll tell yer Pa that ye bate me up!"

The son, angered beyond control, struck the young rogue again and again; but, realizing the trap into which he had been driven, and knowing that his father would, as always, favour Welsh, and that he would probably lose his horse anyhow, decided that discretion was the better part of valour. He handed over the horse and said vindictively:

"Ah hope he breaks yer bloody neck!"

And, in fact, he very nearly did break his neck. A day or two afterwards, as he was forcing the grass-filled animal to gallop up a hill, the horse and he had different ideas: he wished to go in one direction—straight ahead; the colt, on the other hand, wished to go into reverse and, as he couldn't gallop backwards he suddenly spun around in the narrowest possible circle, so that Welsh was pitched forward on his head. Lying there partially stunned, and with a broken collar-bone, he brought down—and up—all the imprecations of heaven and hell on the equine species, and on the whole of mankind excluding himself.

None of these events, however, had the slightest effect on Hugh's preference for the youth who, in his turn, became indispensable. Often Hugh would say to Mrs. Brontë:

"He's a good head on him, that boy."

"Maybe," Mrs. Brontë would reply, "but ye know, Hugh, we can't go on in this way."

"Why not?"

"Have ye no sense, man? Can't ye see the way things are goin'?"

"What do ye mean?"

"Can't ye see that there's never a day passes without a quarrel? Only last week Ah had to separate him and the young fella or they'd a murdhered each other. An' that'll not be the end of it. Oh, Hugh, Hugh ! Why did we ever bring that child home with us ? There's times when Ah think he means more to you than I do."

At this point Mrs. Brontë's feelings got the better of her; and, though this rarely happened to this strong, self-controlled woman, tears began to well up in her eyes and roll gently down her cheeks. An hysterical woman invites anger, but a strong unselfish woman's tears are hard for a husband to bear.

So Brontë, a kindly man by nature, could do none other but put his arm about her as he tried to say consolingly, haltingly:

" No, darlin' woman, he doesn't mean more to me than you; but he's useful. I know how to buy and sell; apart from this I never had much of a head for business. This fella couldn't stand the pace against tough dealers, but he can keep rough accounts, and by God, he's good at knowin' what's in a man's mind. And in consequence we're prosperin'; we're prosperin' all right. You an' I came up the hard way; but look at what our youngsters are gettin': good food, good clothes, good education. There's no knowin' where they may go in the world."

Though he had mollified her, he had not convinced her. Mrs. Brontë felt in her bones that the way they would go would not be the way she and her husband so much desired.

There seems little doubt that the children were reasonably well educated. Where ? I don't know, nor does anybody for that matter; one can merely speculate. Good education was available in Ireland in those days for those who could pay, and for those who professed the Protestant faith. The Royal Schools had been founded, and the Erasmus Smith Schools; two of these, Drogheda and Dundalk Grammar Schools, were near by. Some say the boys were educated in England. Maybe they were; but in any event whether they learned the holy Latin in Drogheda, Dundalk, or the playing fields of Eton, or at Dotheboys Hall matters little, for, as subsequent events were to prove, their knowledge of agriculture and of the buying and selling of cattle did not profit thereby.

When they were away Welsh's opportunities for ingratiat-
ing himself with the master became immeasurably greater.
Moreover, he came to know far too much about the affairs of
the family, which normally would have been the business of
the oldest boy. The pair of them went everywhere together:
to fairs all over Ireland, and with their purchases to sales in
England, which entailed repeated journeys to Liverpool.

Cattle dealing at best—and at worst—is an exacting
occupation requiring the physique and digestion of a rhino-
ceros. How often has one seen little men, big men, lean men,
and fat men standing about in all weathers amid the muck,
mud, and muddle of cows, and cowmen, sheep and sheepmen,
pigs and poultry, and all the other ingredients supposed to
make up the fun of the fair. But there was precious little fun
at Irish cattle fairs in the old days, unless you could observe
them through the eyes of an outsider with a somewhat
sardonic sense of humour, haggling, hand-clapping, drinking
and driving were the order of the day. And when you saw
choleric, and often whiskey-sodden, men with arms and sticks
working like flails, chasing rampaging temper-raising animals,
you wondered how hearts and arteries could withstand such
a strain. They made money—of course they made money—
at least the big men did—and it would have made a tax man's
blood run cold had he thought of the tax evasions and avoid-
ances possible, as he watched the great wads of notes passing
from man to man.

The morning after the big drive was certainly a strain on
Hugh as he shouted:

" Hie there Welsh! Come on boys, ye know what day to-
morrow is; the biggest drove o' cattle ever. They have to be
on the boat before eight. We'll have to have them penned
an' ready to-night. No time to be wasted. Welsh and me
on the horses to find them all ! The rest o' you behind the
bastes. Have your book handy, Welsh, to put down the
numbers. Right boys, get to it ! "

Soon there was the great shouting, yelling, and barking, as the seemingly endless droves of cattle were herded into the pens. This was certainly the biggest cargo of cattle ever to be shipped from Liverpool. For Hugh it was a case of all or bust; all his money was gambled on this last throw of the dice. The cattle must be successfully embarked, and sold in England when the market was at its best.

When Hugh at last got to bed that night for a few hours' sleep before the cattle drive into the dawn he was tired out.

" Take it easy, take it easy man ! " said Mrs. Brontë. " Ye must remember yer gettin' no younger. Leave it to the young fellas. Ah'm worried about that pain in yer chest ye were complainin' of."

" Ah would ye quit yer talkin'," Hugh replied. " Ah'm as fit as men half me age. The pain was nothin' more than a touch o' indigestion. A bottle o' the doctor's physic 'll soon cure that. Ah'll be all right, don't you worry."

But in the morning Hugh's confidence was dispelled, for when he needed all his energy he was assailed by a strange lassitude—something to which he was completely unaccustomed. But the job must be done; he must go ahead at all costs. This was the drove to beat all droves. This was what he had been working for throughout his working life.

In spite of his rebellious body he was here, there and everyshere: goading, cajoling, encouraging, cursing, swearing, running, and in general forcing his body beyond the limits of endurance. At last the job—or at last the first half of it—was done. For years people talked about the drove—perhaps they still talk about it—that swept through the streets of Drogheda like a tidal wave.

When all the cattle were safely impounded aboard ship Hugh repaired to his bunk from which, for the period of the journey, he scarcely stirred. Once or twice Welsh came in with his books and his figures to talk about prices and arrangements for disposal at the other end. But he was met with little more than a disinterested response. He, for his part, showed little sympathy for the tired master who had done so much for him. He had no thought for anything other than possible profits, and how much he could expect for his part in the sale.

The journey passed without incident; and though the morning was cool on arrival in Liverpool, Hugh appeared to be in better spirits after his long rest. The squawking of sea-birds, the cries of sailors, the masts of ships, and the calls of itinerant salesmen along the quayside all had a stimulating effect.

And to crown everything, prices at the sales were the highest on record. So it was that Hugh, with his usual generosity, was able to buy scent and scarves, and souvenirs, hats and hosiery, wines and whiskey, tea and tobacco, and, in fact, everything he could think of to delight the hearts of his men and womenfolk.

The excitement over, he felt unusually tired once more; and there was that terrible feeling of tightness and the pain across his chest. Soon after going on board he went down to his bunk; a couple of hours later his soul had gone to his particular paradise: no doubt among luscious fields filled with fat cattle.

CHAPTER 4

HOME-COMINGS

IT was dark that evening when a messenger arrived from Drogheda. He asked if he could speak to Mrs. Brontë. Certainly, would he just step inside. As he appeared to be a man of good address and appearance one of the girls ushered him into the room at the end of the house usually reserved for visitors; as Papa was expected home that evening a great log fire was blazing on the hearth, and the first roses of summer were adding their scent to those one usually associates with a country house.

"Just wait here a minute," said one of the girls, "while I call Mama."

Was it intuition, or the look and demeanour of her husband before his departure, that made Mrs. Brontë know what had happened, almost before the messenger spoke to her?

"I'm sorry, madam. I—I—I'm afraid I . . ."

But before he could get the words out of his mouth Mrs. Brontë said:

"Oh, I know, I know. I knew it all the time. When Hugh left me here I felt it was for the last time. . . . I knew I would never see him again."

"Oh, God! my Hugh, my Hugh! How'll I ever do without him? Oh, God, why have ye done this to me? He was such a good, kind, and generous man. We'll all miss him so—everyone of us."

As in all such cases, the harbinger of bad tidings felt himself very much at a loss. He scarcely knew what to say; and so he ended up with the usual trite remarks: time, the great healer, would eventually help her to forget; no doubt

25

her family would be a great consolation; they had many friends who would rally round to help her. . . . All very true, no doubt, but useless to a woman suffering from bereavement's initial, numbing shock. She felt dazed; and, for the time being, incapable of coherent thought.

One by one the various members of the family came to know what had happened. Without her better half the mother felt she was only half with them, but as each one kissed her, and their grief mingled with hers, she began to feel so warmed by their affection that she calmed down somewhat. Then, like many women in such circumstances, her accustomed practicality began to assert itself. Suddenly, as her mind cleared, she said:

" Where's Welsh ? "

But nobody had seen him; nobody had seen him from the time the ship docked. He had apparently slipped away under cover of darkness. So the messenger said; and he also intimated quietly to some of the boys that the ship's captain was insisting that the body should be removed forthwith:

Mrs. Brontë's grief had now turned to anger.

" I always knew it," she moaned, " I always knew that fella was no good; that sooner or later he would let us all down. Now when he's most needed he's not here; and we don't know who to turn to. What are we to do ? "

The boys, of course, insisted that, though the hour was late, they would drive down to the docks forthwith to see what arrangements could be made. Without further ado they set out; and were eventually able to find an undertaker who would do all that was necessary. He would bring home the embalmed, en-coffined body first thing the following morning; and he would make all arrangements for the funeral. In the meantime the boys were allowed to see, and identify, their father, and also to search his clothes and luggage for any personal belongings. Apart from the gifts, and spare clothes, they found nothing—absolutely nothing; all trace of records and the vast sum of money that should have been on his person or in his baggage had completely disappeared.

It was significant that Welsh had also disappeared. Why? Obviously because he had taken the money and destroyed the records. Why did somebody not go after him? People can disappear without trace in our own day, let alone when there were neither telegraphs nor telephones, neither police, nor newspapers, and in a heavily-wooded, heavily-populated countryside open to the sea, and its plying ships. In such circumstances a man with money in his pockets could disappear if he so wished, and no questions would be asked.

The following morning, with the whole countryside in the full flush and bloom of its summer beauty, the sad little cortège proceeded from Drogheda docks through the cattle-dotted dales of the Boyne valley for Hugh's last homecoming to the farm which he had loved, and where he was loved. For the next few days all was fuss and bustle. One is inclined to think that an Irish wake is a Catholic tradition; but this isn't so, or at least, if it were originally so, then the tradition rubbed off on well-established Protestant families also. Indeed the writer remembers the term being used quite often by Protestants in the countryside of the County Down.

Be that as may be, friends and neighbours flocked in for the next day or two; and there was no time for sobs or tears. Mrs. Brontë and the girls were kept so busy cutting, cooking, and dish washing, that they had little rest or respite from dawn to dusk. The amount of ham and jam, bread and wine, whiskey and tobacco consumed was not only a tribute to Hugh's popularity, but also it indicated the healthy country appetites of the sympathizers.

At last it was all over. The remains of Hugh had been safely committed; and the business of living had to be resumed. It was apparent that the farm alone could not sustain the family. It had been neglected. In those early eighteenth-century days little was known about the scientific side of agriculture. You grazed a field until it was exhausted, and then you moved to another, leaving it to nature's slow hand to bring about the necessary restoration. When a field became so choked with weeds that grass could no longer compete, you hoped that sheep or goats, or other change of cattle not so selective as the bovine species, would do all that was necessary. Effective methods when time and money were no object, but quite impractical when it was necessary to restore quickly the family fortunes.

As in many farming families the boys were completely unfamiliar with the business side of farming. While they could read, write, and ride, shoot fish, and mix well with country and county, there it ended. They could neither buy nor sell, nor indeed had they sufficient knowledge of the land to make good general farmers. What was the result ? The once green acres had become rush-filled, fern-filled and moss-filled, and completely unproductive, both for cattle and crops. Ireland at this time was suffering one of those famine periods which were to weaken almost permanently its finances, its manhood, and its womanhood. The harvest failure throughout the country as a whole had its repercussions even on the Brontë farm; this combined with the family's local problem served to accentuate more acutely the disastrous loss of the head of the house.

When local gossip had it that Welsh had been seen around feelings were mixed. Mrs. Brontë said:

" I forbid that man ever to enter this house again ! "

" Listen, Mama," said one of the boys, " it's all very well for you to say that, an' God knows none of us want him here, but the fact of the matter is, we can't do without him. He knows more about the workin' o' the place than any o' the rest of us. Besides he must have the money; an' ye know the rent's been owin' for some time. Ye know as well as we do what that means. Only last week Paddy Quinn was thrown out lock, stock and barrel. The agents are taking every advantage of the situation to gain control of the land."

Most of the family were on the side of their mother. Few, except the most pragmatic, wished to see the man about the place again.

" Good riddance ! " one said, " he's gone now, let's keep him out no matter what happens. It was he who killed poor Papa and brought all our present troubles on us."

" Don't we know all that; but that's not the point," one of the others expostulated, " let him come back until we get things straightened out, then we'll throw him out again. After all, he never considered us, why should we consider him?"

" No ! No ! No ! " Mrs. Brontë said, for once showing signs of temper. " I just couldn't stand him here. If he comes in I'm going out; and then ye can do what ye want."

And so they argued and argued, some of the boys—and the girls for that matter—almost coming to blows. Only Mary, curiously red in the face, kept silence. But then, as her mother said, " You never knew what was going on in the mind of that girl."

In the end the more practical members managed to persuade their mother, and the other dissenters, that after all it might be in their best interests to have the man back, at least for a period, and until such time as there was enough cash in hands to invest in the former business of buying and selling cattle. Though Mrs. Brontë agreed, it was with reluctance. She had never liked Welsh as a child, a boy, or as he now was, a grown man. Though not normally superstitious by nature, she was, after all, a product of her country, her day, and her age. Few at this time would have dismissed the idea that some people's bodies were inhabited, if not by evil spirits, at least by the spirit of evil. Every time she had any dealings with Welsh she had this feeling about him. Deep down in her heart she knew that, as surely as night followed day, his return would—or could—bring tragedy and sorrow.

Scarcely had the discussion ended when a message arrived from Welsh requesting a meeting with all available members of the family at the earliest possible moment. He had something important to discuss with them. The more trusting of the little community concluded that he had the money and books in his safe keeping, and that he hoped to be able to return these conditionally. Possibly he might ask to be reinstated as a member of the family with his former status restored. Only Mary, as usual, reddened and looked somewhat taken aback. The remainder, with reservations, were prepared to accept the inevitable.

Based on the incontrovertible assumption that there is no time like the present, each and all decided that the interview should take place without delay. Accordingly word was sent back that the family were assembled and waiting, and would Mr. Welsh make the journey to the farm post-haste.

But there was a delay—a considerable delay—during which the anxieties, apprehensions, and tempers of those present rose to fever pitch. Whether we are on one side of a desk or the other, most of us throughout our lives have had painful interviews. If we are in the seat of authority we may not like the person we are about to interview. On the other hand if we are the person being interviewed, we might well be fearful of the interviewer. Sensing this state of mind the probabilities are that Welsh, with his accustomed sinister shrewdness, deliberately delayed his arrival, so as to wear to shreds the already taut nerves of most of the members of the family.

" What was that noise ? " someone said. " Ah, there he is at last ! " The clop of horses' feet suddenly ceased; and there was the sound of wheels grinding to a halt. Before anyone had time to open the door the door was thrown open and there stood Welsh on the threshold.

May gave a little gasp; and somebody said: " My God ! "

CHAPTER 5

MARRIAGE WITHOUT CONSENT

T HE exclamations of surprise soon changed to titters and suppressed laughter, for the sight that met their gaze was almost farcical. Here was the young fellow they had always known and despised dressed, as Mrs. Brontë said to a friend later, " up to the ninety-nines ! " His black gleaming broadcloth and greasy black hair served to accentuate more than ever the sallow colour, prominent teeth, and evil eyes. Moreover, he had arrived in a horse-drawn chaise, the like of which had rarely been seen in that part of the country. Obviously everything had been done to impress.

With pomposity and thinly-veiled contempt he glanced around the room, momentarily fixing his gaze on Mary, who blushed and quickly withdrew her eyes. He said:

" Sorry about the old man, ye know, but these things happen. You at least, Mrs. Brontë, have the satisfaction of knowing he died without pain. Most unfortunate ! Most unfortunate ! But after all worse things can happen; he could have been gored by a savage beast or run down by a horse. Still it's bound to have been a shock, and you all have my sympathy."

" Farm doing all right ? Difficult without the boss ! If there's anything I can do to help . . ."

At this point one of the more quick-tempered boys stood up with menacing fists.

" Where's our father's money, ye bastard ? "

" All right, now, all right," said the unruffled Welsh. " How should I know anything about yer father's money ? These ships, ye know, they're full of all sorts of rogues and villains—always on the look-out for such an opportunity. Yer father was robbed when I went up to see the captain. I cleared out because I thought I'd be accused."

" Had one or two lucky breaks myself; saved a bit ye know an' did a bit o' buyin' and sellin' on me own. If ye need a bit o' spare cash say the word."

Though no one believed this story, nothing could be proved, so mother and all the others remained silent.

Then Welsh dropped his bombshell.

" Now, look here," he said, " Ah'll tell ye what Ah'm prepared to do. Ah'll come back here an' look after things on one condition: the condition is that Mary 'll marry me."

" Ye'll what ! Marry our Mary ! Not on yer life ! If ye as much as try to lay a hand on that girl Ah'll murder ye ! " said one of the brothers.

In a moment there was pandemonium. Another brother looked as if he were about to strike down Welsh with a hammer blow of his fist. One of the girls screamed; another sobbed. Only Mrs. Brontë kept her head and besought everybody to be quiet and calm. She looked at Welsh with scorn and disdain; in a quiet voice she said:

" Get out of this house and never darken our doors again ! We need neither your help nor your money. I can trust my own boys to do all that's needful to restore our fortunes. Get out ! I say, get out ! "

Welsh took up his hat and prepared to leave, but before doing so he faced the whole company, and said in a way that struck fear into all of them:

" Mary shall yet be my wife; and I will scatter the rest of you like chaff from this house which shall be my house."

The family now knew that the sword was out of the scabbard; that from now on it would be a fight to a finish to prevent this rascal from destroying them. After what amounted to a council of war, it was decided that some of the family should go out into the world to make whatever money they could, whilst those who could not be spared would do everything they could to restore the land to its original state of fertility. In the meantime there must be economies: the hired hands would have to go.

As it turned out the Brontës did not scatter like chaff before the wind. It would be true, however, to say that some went under their own power; that these, with the help of influential friends, were able to become established and prosperous, appears to be certain; thus they were in due time able to follow the good old Irish custom of sending money home to help the home farm. There were good neighbours, too, who helped with the digging, ploughing, harrowing and sowing, all of which was so necessary to bring the farm back into production. Every domestic and agricultural art and skill were practised so as to make the home self-sufficient, while at the same time turning as much as possible into cash to further future operations.

When I was a boy I was led to believe that hard work and application were the main requirements for success in life. If this dictum were ever true, it was certainly not true in the Ireland of the eighteenth century when a well-improved farm was an irresistible carrot in the eyes of agents and sub-agents. These often unscrupulous men, to curry favour with absentee landlords and line their own pockets, would raise the rent further and further to an extent that the unfortunate tenant sooner or later was unable to pay—the result: eviction.

Now it so happened that Welsh was still in the district; with characteristic cunning he wangled his way into the job of sub-agent—a post for which he was eminently suited. There may be reasons why every man becomes what he is: inborn temperament, environment, a chip on the shoulder-as we say-induced by unhappy circumstances in childhood. No doubt such influences were at work on the mind of this man. Whatever excuses we may make for him, or whatever reasons we may adduce as to why he had such an unfortunate character, the fact remains that he was calculating, ruthless, selfish, and pityless—at least toward the family which had given him shelter and sustenance. Possibly there were faults on both sides, and possibly he was actuated by that strange perversity which causes some to hate those to whom they owe most.

He was the sort of man who would go into a pub and, while drinking very little himself, he would encourage any talkative client to drink as much as possible.

" Come on, man, have another one, an' give us a bit o' yer ould crack," he would say. " Here, drink up, sure 'tis terrible slow ye are." Then when he thought the man's tongue was properly loosened there would be one or two salacious stories, or maybe the current gossip about local girls of doubtful reputation. The form of girls would be talked about in much the same way as the form of horses.

" That young filly; she's a high jumper all right," Welch would say, drawing closer to the man and becoming more confidential.

" As for that one in the cottage above, she'd lie down on any bed—or for that matter on any bank "—this with a sly wink from Welsh.

" Ah'm told the place up there's goin' to rack and ruin; it wouldn't graze a goat let alone a head o' cattle. Ah believe she's other means o' raisin' the money for the rent." This was just the information Welsh wanted.

" Ye don't tell me ! " Welsh would reply, looking suitably shocked, while at the same time making a mental note of facts to be supplied to the landlord forthwith.

" Nice lot o' wenches up at the Brontë place; Ah wonder how they're gettin' on these days."

" Ah don't know much about them. Ye don't see them around much—not at the barn dances, nor dancin' down at the Cross; but they're purty all right. That Mary one, now she's a deep, dark horse if ever there was one. Not a lad in the country wouldn't give his right hand for her."

" Ah hear they're working away hard up there," the man continued, " tryin' to make a go of the place, but it's uphill work; an' without the cattle Ah can't see much prospect for them."

Such conversations made Welsh realize there was no time to be wasted. His madness for Mary was compounded of two insensate desires: lust for Mary and lust for land. He would have her at all costs. His instincts led him to believe that she was attracted, physically at least, toward him; and he knew that physical desire, when powerful enough, can sometimes prompt indiscretion, even on the part of the most discreet.

One day one of the boys came in with a note delivered by a messenger from the land agent:

" Listen to this," said he, " the bugger has raised our rent ! "

The others said, their language being no better than those around them:

" Hell damn and blast him ! Some informer has told him that we're making improvements ! "

" And you haven't very far to look for the informer," said the mother, " but we'll not be beaten by him or by anyone else. We'll pay the extra rent, and we'll go ahead."

And they went ahead. Letters were sent to the brothers in Ireland and in England; they responded to a man, sending home increased amounts of money to offset the rent increase. Efforts on the farm were redoubled.

Soon there was another demand, and another, and yet another, until it seemed that sooner or later the position would become intolerable. But greater and greater efforts were made on the part of the family, both at home and abroad. The rent was paid on the nail each time; thus, as there were no grounds for eviction, there was no eviction.

Becoming more and more chagrined, Welsh decided on other tactics. He meant to marry Mary anyhow, but not by putting the cart before the horse. Now he decided to do just this: he would marry Mary first, and gain possession afterwards. His ruse was simple: have Mary importuned in such a way that she would have no recourse other than to accept his hand in marriage.

There is—or was—in every Irish district an old creature who has become an almost legendary figure. She is often squat; she wears a shawl; and not infrequently she smokes " an ould clay." Her eyes are wicked and beady, and she usually has a high-pitched squeaky voice. She prophesises everything from the sex of an unborn child to the chances of the next harvest being good or bad. She lives in an old tumbledown thatch cottage, and in summer-time she is often to be seen squatting, smoking, and contemplating, under the shelter of a hedge. She may greet you with a " top o' the mornin', sir," and will as often as not offer to read your hand or the tea-cup. Some specialize in one direction, and others in another direction. Some may advise frightened girls on how to get rid of an unwanted child, or indeed on how to avoid having a child; others might even take greater risks. Some, in the past, carried on a remunerative trade in passing on illegitimate children for upbringing in homes, both legal and illegal. Not a few would, for a consideration, arrange marriages, especially in cases where a little pressure had to be brought to bring one partner or the other up to scratch. These women were often feared, not only because they frequently knew too much about apparently respectable people, but also because ordinary simple folk regarded them as possessing some degree of witchcraft.

Such a one was Meg. What a fitting accomplice for the thwarted, twisted Welsh ! Her reputation had gone far and wide. Of all of her tribe she was the most unscrupulous. She would trade in anything: whiskey for alcoholic women, charms for the avoidance of children, eggs—stolen or otherwise—in exchange for ornaments, women for the pleasure of men and, above all, she would, without conscience, supply all the information necessary to have good people driven from their homes into outer darkness.

A meeting was arranged. Aye ! aye ! she would, for a consideration, endeavour to further Welsh's suit with Mary. Gently at first of course; a well brought up girl like her must be brought on gently. No rough measures—a word now and again—flowers maybe—trinkets and ornaments—good clean clothes—an impression of wealth and prosperity—a gentlemanly approach. When the unsuspecting girl had been softened, up rougher methods might be tried to bring about the final show-down.

Was Mary antagonistic or protagonistic ? Only she knew that, for there is no record to indicate that anyone saw her with Welsh before the end of the affair. As in *Wuthering Heights* was there any Penistone Crag around the high-banked Boyne where these two met clandestinely ? We don't know. And yet, events that followed might lead the suspicious-minded to suspect.

There are few charming girls oblivious of their charms. There are few unaware of the attentions and compliments offered by the opposite sex. There are many rebellious spirits attracted toward men who, because of an unsavoury reputation, are spoken of in whispers. Maybe things are different in our so-called permissive age, but in days when women rarely got away from home's cloying comforts, it was not unusual to jump the barriers of convention toward those who offered love's release in less conventional and more licentious forms.

Thus the flowers, the trinkets, the trivialities, and compliments that found their way to Mary's possession and heart must have caused some response. If not, why did she not, once and for all, block the avenue from which these proceeded ? And of course Miss Meg was the go-between. Mary must have met her; she must have known about her wicked reputation; she must have complied to some extent—possibly against the dictates of reason and common sense.

Now Welsh appeared to be highly prosperous. He went about in the grand manner in a borrowed carriage. He adopted the manners, dress, and general demeanour of a local squireen.

He knew that stories of all this, often exaggerated, would inevitably be reported back to the Brontës. We sometimes talk as though status symbols, money-lust and desire for power were diseases of our own day; this is arrant nonsense. The desire to impress is a deep-seated instinct of the human kind; and wherever and whenever the two sexes become involved, this instinct becomes sharpened an hundredfold. This cock-in-the-barnyard behaviour on the part of Welsh was largely inspired by his wish to conquer Mary by means fair or foul. Once having won her, he knew it would be but a short step to his final goal—the securing of the Brontë home and property.

One day he and Meg met in the local inn. Whiskey in hand she sidled up to him and said in her cracked, wheezy, voice, and with a leer on her face:

" Oi tink, me dear, the fruit's ready for the pluckin'. She's prepared to meet ye."

" Good," said Welsh, showing excitement for once. " When ? Where ? "

" Ah, now, don't get too excited, or ye might spoil things. She's a tender flower, me dear, it would be all too aisy to crush her. Go aisy, go aisy, all in good time."

" But," said she, coming closer to him so that he could smell the tobacco and the whiskey breath, " it would take another pound or two to buy one or two more love charms."

Seeing the look of reluctance on his face, she wheedled him still further. " Ah, now," she went on, " ye wouldn't spoil the ship for a ha'p'orth o' tar, would ye ? An', after all, what's a poun' or two to a man with your purse ? Eh ! "

" Here ye are," Welsh said irritably. " Now get on with it for God's sake."

" Now, now, calm down," the woman said. " This'll make a power o' difference. Oi'll tell ye what I'll do: there'll be a full moon to-morrow night—the right time for love makin'," she leered. " Oi'll get her to slip out afther supper on the pretext that she has a bit o' a headache; and she'd like to get out for a while in the fresh air to let it blow away the cobwebs. You be in the clearin' in the wood a mile or so above the house; and depind on it I'll not be very far away. If she denies anything afterwards it might be as well to have a witness."

He was not particularly partial to such an arrangement, but he at once saw the practical necessity. Though in his peculiar cold way he was in love with Mary, the ultimate success of his scheme must depend on some form of legal marriage.

What Meg said to Mary, or how in the end she managed to persuade her to meet Welsh in the wood is not recorded. One can merely conclude that Mary required little persuasion. She was, after all, young, passionate, and untutored in the ways of the world of men; and this one—the one she was to meet—had been known to her all her life. Sometimes she had regarded him with pity because he was an outcast, sometimes with scorn because of his alien ways; but in her times of clear-minded honesty she had to admit to herself that her feelings toward him were not without passion.

Thus it came about that on that clear, clean September night she slipped out; skipped over the stimulating dewy grass; and, keeping away from view from the house from which she could have been clearly seen silhouetted in the silver light of the September moon, she was soon at the ferney fringe of the wood. Once inside the comforting leafiness she was, as *she* thought, safe from observation; but there were two eyes watching her as stealthily as a cat watching a bird.

As she proceeded toward the clearing her thoughts became more and more confused. Was she walking into a trap? She knew this man was devoid of kindliness, good nature, and the refinements she had been taught to look for and respect. What did she want to do with him now? No sooner did such a thought come into her mind than she felt half-thrilled by it. Should she turn back now before it was too late? Yes, she would turn back; she even made a half-turn only to find that her feet were impelled forward by some force outside her control. Then she saw him waiting for her in the moss-covered clearing. She ran forward straight into his waiting arms.

An hour later, as they lay on the moss together, Welsh, with neither sentiment nor affection, said:

" You'll have to marry me now you know: to all intents and purposes we're already man and wife." At this juncture nothing was said about the hidden witness. " However, apart altogether from what has taken place between us, I'd rather you'd say *yes* of your own free will. What about it then? Will you marry me?"

" Yes," she replied simply and without endearment.

" All right, then," Welsh said, " I'll make whatever arrangements are necessary; but remember it'll all have to be simple and secret. Nothing must be said until it's too late for any of the family to object."

In the meantime the crestfallen, secretive Mary sang no songs, sad or otherwise, about the house. Though she had always been quiet, apart from the fact that, as somebody said, she could almost silence the birds with her singing, now she appeared pale, wan, and haggard. If this period—the time before her marriage, and the explosion that must result from the announcement—had gone on for long she would probably have become ill.

Time dragged on; for Mary weeks seemed like months, then one day she had a message to say that she was to meet Welsh in the clearing once more, this time in the presence of a witness, and a buckle-rigger who could legitimately perform the marriage. There must be absolute secrecy; she was not even to put a ribbon in her hair; she must dress exactly as she would have done on any normal day. Never was a girl to be married in less glamorous, or more unromantic, circumstances. How often she regretted her stupid action, prompted partly by passion; and partly by the fear of this man who could have ruined her family—at least so she had been led to believe. But there was no turning back now.

To allay the effects of superstition, and to be in accord with the law, she must be married in the morning; and to ensure that nobody would be around the event was to take place on the Fair Day. As it happened the day also was fair and beautiful. As the girl made her way up again to the clearing she couldn't help noticing the reddening leaves adding their burning glory to the lovely Boyne Valley. How she wished that things could have been different ! How she wished that this happiest day in the life of most girls could have been a truly happy day for her. But it was not to be: for her no gossamer gown, no bouquet of autumn blooms no feasting, no dancing, no joy. Like all the rest of us she could see no further than the immediate moment. She did not know the inscrutable ways of whatever power directs the universe; she couldn't have known that if it hadn't been for this apparently unwise action of hers, one of the greatest literary families in history might never have come into being.

And so a few more steps and she was into the dark cover of the woods, and then into the brilliant light of the clearing; there on this moss-covered bank was the only marriage altar she would ever know. The only witnesses were the wheezy mendacious Meg, and the down-at-heel buckle-begger. Of course the groom was dressed for the part. From his shiny buckled shoes to his equally shiny hair, he was immaculate, as befitted one who was soon to become a gentleman of property—at least so he thought.

It was sad to observe the dissolution of a family; it is sadder to see the dissolution of an Irish country family in the circumstances about to be witnessed, and which have often been witnessed. A son and heir, or a daughter and heiress bring a cuckoo into the nest just when those who have worked for the place all their lives are beginning to see some results from their labours. Often the whole place becomes the property

D

of the newcomer with the result that the father, the mother, and any others are left virtually destitute.

Judge the horror and fear there must have been in the hearts and minds of the Irish family Brontë when Mary came home with her wedding ring on her appropriate finger, and her inappropriate detested new husband at her side. They just couldn't believe it. They were dumbfounded.

At least one of the brothers, finding his voice, shouted:

" Get to hell out of it the two o' ye and never darken these doors again ! "

Before anyone could stay his hand he rushed, and pushing his sister out of the way, he struck Welsh such a blow that he knocked him through the half-door with blood streaming from his face.

Welsh made no attempt to retaliate, he simply rose to his feet, wiped his mouth with his kerchief; and with malevolence written all over his countenance, he informed his antagonist that now that Mary was his wife he was taking over the tenancy. They would be duly informed by the agent within the next few days.

That Welsh held the whip hand was now obvious. The mother, as usual, calmed the situation. Though she would be the heaviest loser, and could only look forward to unhappy years when she would no longer be mistress in her own house, she put her arms around her sobbing daughter and said:

" You are my daughter, Mary. I'll always do my best to make life as happy as possible for you."

Mary, not very articulate at the best of times, was so overcome by her feelings that she was quite unable to reply, and could only throw her arms about her stricken mother. Later, however, she confided the whole story to Mrs. Brontë who, with the sure instinct of a good mother and a woman, understood Mary's terrible predicament.

In due course the bribed agent himself arrived at the farm.

" How do you do, Mrs. Brontë ? " he said, with pompous courtesy. " I regret very much the occasion for this visit. It is, however, my unpleasant duty to have to inform you that you are no longer the tenant of this farm; and I am to ask you to sign this document which indicates the same, and states that from this day the rightful tenant will be your son-in-law Mr. Welsh Brontë."

Poor Mrs. Brontë ! What could she do ? She knew nothing of the law. All she could say was that her son-in-law had no right to call himself Welsh Brontë. He was no more Brontë than the agent. He was a foundling brat; she and her husband had taken pity on him when they found him on board ship; they had brought him home, fed, clothed, educated him, and given him a home through the years. This was a poor return for all they had done.

" Well," said the agent with unction, " if you did all that, it was an acknowledgment of the fact that you had accepted him as a foster-son. This fully entitled him to assume the name Brontë; and I might add that he has legalized the situation by having his name registered as Welsh Brontë."

Mrs. Brontë signed the document feeling as though she were signing her death warrant—maybe she was; no doubt such transactions and troubles would have hastened her end.

Though the family were to be scattered, they were not scattered like chaff before the wind, for chaff puts up no resistance, whereas the Brontës fought this villanous brother-in-law to the last ditch. They all returned to fight their case before a magistrate, but as the magistrate proved to be the agent the result was a foregone conclusion.

When all else failed they foolishly took the law into their own hands. Armed with whatever weapons were available—sticks, cudgels, and such like—they advanced upon the farm one evening:

" Come out ! " they shouted. " Come out and take yer medicine ye dirty welsher; this is our home an' here we're goin' to stay ! Come out to hell, before we burn ye out ! "

But they were no match for the wary Welsh. He had anticipated the attack. They were arrested, tried, and sentenced to imprisonment with hard labour. The magistrate—the agent again—was very sorry for what had happened; but, they had only themselves to blame. Whatever the circum-stances, and as a private individual he had the greatest sympathy for Mrs. Brontë and the family, the law must be upheld. "Here was a man, fully entitled—I repeat fully entitled—to the property under his control; he has guaranteed to restore the property to its full potential, and to offer house and home to Mrs. Brontë and the girls for as long as they wish to remain. He has acted in an honourable and chivalrous manner. What more could be expected of him ? You, on the other hand, by your senseless, violent actions have aligned yourselves with those who have always been the curse of this country. I sentence you to prison with hard labour. . . ."

And so Welsh, like the Heathcliff of Emily's imagination, found himself in full possession of all that he had craved for since his overmastering obsession had taken hold of him.

What happened later must for ever remain enshrouded in the mists of obscurity. After their release the brothers went their ways. They prospered in a world in which hard work and courage were sometimes the qualities leading to ultimate success. The girls left home, possibly to go into service, to get married, or to do both. As for Mrs. Brontë, she went to live with one of the family, where one hopes she found some rest for mind and body before she went—as she would have put it—to join her husband.

CHAPTER 6

BLACK NIGHTS AND BLEAK DAYS

A T last one of the Brontës must have attained a considerable
measure of prosperity. The same member of the family
must also have possessed a rare capacity for forgiveness. Not
everybody can forgive a minor hurt or insult, let alone one
that has cut into the whole fabric of their lives. But the
brother, father of young Hugh, must have been an unusual
man in this respect. And his prosperity appears to have made
him think with some sentimentality and nostalgia about the
old home on the banks of the Boyne.

Surely he harboured ideas that at some time or other
he would return as the owner, or that at least one of his
sons would be able to take the place over. This is, of course,
mere conjecture, but it is conjecture based on fact. How
otherwise can one explain his decision to enter into a bargain with
the man who came into possession by such nefarious means?
Either that, or Welsh had such a smooth, glib tongue that
he could almost hypnotize people into carrying out his
wishes. On the other hand it could have been that young
Hugh's father had a somewhat misplaced faith in his sister
Mary; he may have thought that she had sufficient power
over her husband to be able to keep him from further wrong-
doing.

Though details had not yet been settled, he had some notion
of what was pending one day when a smart enough cart and
horse drew up at his door.

" God save all here ! Anybody in ? " said a voice.

" Aye, there's somebody in; an' what would ye be
wantin' ? " was the reply.

" Do ye not recognize me ? 'Tis Welsh, an' here's your sister Mary come to see ye."

Ignoring Welsh the brother rushed into the arms of the sister—the favourite, the one he had always loved best. Looking deeply into her eyes he saw there no well of happiness. The only well was of tears that brimmed gently. They were tears of relief at seeing one of the family again.

The brother said:

" You have no youngsters of your own ? "

" No—not one. What wouldn't I give for a child ? What about yours; are they well ? "

" Och aye, they're all fine; come in ! come in ! and meet herself and the youngsters."

The children stood around shyly as Aunt Mary and Uncle Welsh were introduced.

" What a healthy, happy-looking lot," said Mary. " Would you not give me one of them ? "

Mary and the wife took to each other at once. Mary wanted to know all about the children: their ages, their health, which were the best-behaved, which were like their mother, which like their father; in fact they quickly became engrossed in the usual conversation between two married women.

At first the youngsters didn't take to Welsh at all; later, however, he went out of his way to make himself agreeable to them; he joined in their games; he bought them sweets, toys, and trinkets in the local shop. He so ingratiated himself with them that they soon came to think that this business of having visitors was good fun. He made a great fuss of Hugh, then about six years old. He told him all about the home farm, about all the animals they had, about the shooting, the fishing, and particularly about the ponies for riding. Altogether he had the child so buoyed up that he asked if he could go home with his Aunt Mary and Uncle Welsh.

" Please ! please ! " he said, " please take me home with you ! "

This was all in accordance with plan. That night the two men, over glasses of whiskey and pipes of tobacco, were more relaxed. Indeed Welsh became almost maudlin in his expressions of sorrow about all that had happened. He was now a changed man; Mary's love had worked wonders with him. He explained that in his earlier years, knowledge of his origins had made him feel so inferior that he had to take it out of other people. This had caused him to do things that he knew to be wrong, and yet he found it impossible to control himself.

" Ah, now," said the naturally good-natured Brontë, " would ye quit talkin', sure I know we didn't always treat ye too well. Ye see, young spalpeens are terrible bullies; an' they're always liable to make a set on those who are different. Sure we'll let bygones be bygones."

" You're very kind to me, man, kinder than I deserve," replied the two-faced Welsh. " Mebbe all that happened was for the best anyhow. Ye deserve great credit. Look at the place ye have here. You and your good wife, have the blessing of children. What wouldn't Mary and I give to have a toddler on two about the place. And mind you it would be a great place for youngsters. Between you and me we've made a great job of it. I've been workin' a bit at the dealin' meself; an' with the money Ah've made we've been able to repair the house an' improve the land. Now the grass is supportin' cows, horses, and bastes of every description. But what's the use of it all without an heir ? "

" Aye, right enough," Brontë said, with the overriding thought in his mind that, if he were to hand over one of the children, the property would eventually come back to the family. Besides, the wife hadn't been too well of late; she looked tired; perhaps with one less to look after it would be a help.

" Aye ! aye ! " he continued, " there's Hughie now, a bright strong wee fella. We'd miss him o' course, but if ye'd promise to look after him well, and to see that he got the best possible education, we might be prepared to consider the matter."

Before Brontë had time to change his mind Welsh jumped at the offer. Out shot his hand. " Yer han' on it," he said, "o' course he'll be well looked after. Ye know yer sister, Mary, the best woman in the world."

After more bargaining the deal was clinched on oath. The boy would be handed over body and soul to his foster-parents, never again to see his real parents—an arrangement not unusual in the Ireland of those days.

Why didn't Mary speak out? Why didn't she let the Brontës know the true state of affairs? Fear of her tyrannical husband? The desperate urge for a child? The undying hope that sooner or later her partner would become a different man? Probably all three thoughts were operating consciously, or unconsciously, in her mind. Anyhow, and for whatever reason, she did not speak out; and she did not let the Brontës know the true state of affairs. Indeed things could not have been much worse; they were appalling.

One can only guess at what went on between herself and Welsh. His failure to make anything of the cattle dealing, the continual shortage of money, the deterioration of the farm, and above all, his failure to give her a child, were in themselves sufficient reasons for bad marital relationships. Because of his job as sub-agent with its consequent sycophantic attitude toward the agent, he was heartily disliked and socially ostra-cized by the peasant people, who rightly saw him as the instrument of evictions and other suppressions of their rights. One night he was overtaken by Nemesis. She came down out of the hills in the form of an avenging rabble. The leaders told him to come out to hell out o' that and all with him, or they would burn him out. Though the agent was assassinated that night, Mary and Welsh made their escape to the clearing in which they had been married.

But this did not prevent the incendiarists from performing their vengeful task; and, as Welsh and Mary, hiding in the cover of the friendly trees, watched, they saw the last of the Brontë possessions reduced to their elements in a fiery conflag-ration which, as somebody said afterwards, "bate the light o' the moon itself." For Mary it was God's punishment for their sins, but for Welsh it was a further incitement to get even with the antagonistic world into which he had been hurled by a malignant fate.

Fifty pounds was to be paid for the upkeep and education of Hugh. Fifty pounds ! When his father heard this he nearly withdrew from the arrangement. Fifty pounds in those days represented a considerable sum of money. Indeed if the boy had been sent to a good boarding school the fees could not have been much higher. As for Hugh's mother, she disliked the whole arrangement for she loved the wee boy. How could she have agreed ? One must remember that those were the days of families unlimited; other children might soon be on the way. She was persuaded that it was for the boy's own good; and it was an opportunity for him eventually to come into his rightful inheritance.

" Come on now, Hughie, stand up on the chair ! " said the dressmaker who had just made and fitted the suit in which Hugh was to go away.

" Stand up there, while I give you the *beverage* kiss." This was the kiss given to the wearer of new clothes as a token of good luck.

Obediently Hugh did as he was bid; he stood up on the chair so that the dressmaker was able to throw her arms around him; and give him as big a hug and kiss as he had ever had from anybody. " God bless and keep ye," said she with tears brimming in her eyes. The good lady appeared to have sensed the fact that all was not well; and that the little boy would need all the luck that anybody could wish for him.

One by one the brothers and sisters hugged him and said good-bye—and then the mother: the sudden cleavage between the mother and her little son was almost like the breaking of the umbilical cord for the second time. She held him very close to her as she called him " My sweet flower "; but he did not respond. He suddenly felt manly; he didn't want all this sentiment. After all he was going away on a great adventure; he was going away to where there would be horses and dogs, and all the other joys of uninhibited country life. For him it

was to be a happy holiday. He knew nothing of those waves
of homesickness on which many of us would have been
caught up, even in reasonably propitious circumstances, and
even when we had travelled further on life's journey than a
mere six years.

But when Hugh was heaved up to the cross-seat of the
cart on a dark and cold night, at a time when he would
normally have been in in his warm bed, he did't feel so happy.
However, he soon made the best of things by snuggling in
close to his Aunt Mary who, in her turn, had never felt so
happy in her life as she did now with her arms close around
her new wee son.

Children who talk a lot and listen well are usually intelligent
children. Hugh did both; as they rattled along in the uncomfortable cart, sleep being denied him, and a night drive being
a new experience, he was full of questions about where they
were going, about what it would be like when they reached
home, about the moon and about the stars in the night sky.
When we say he had a sudden and rude awakening we are not
saying what the phrase implies in a literal sense. Suddenly,
without warning, the hitherto kind uncle gave him a clout
that nearly knocked him out of the cart.

" If ye don't shut yer wee mouth, ye young whelp, Ah'll
throw ye out on the road, an' leave ye there ! " shouted
Welsh in a voice that Hugh scarcely recognized.

At once Mary held the boy closer to her. " How could
you do such a thing, an' him only a wee boy just out of his
mother's arms ? "

" Shut up the two o' ye, or Ah'll leave ye both on the
roadside ! " Welsh replied as he vented his feeling on the
unfortunate horse, which he whipped without mercy. Not
only had his suppressed ill-nature come violently to the
surface after the few days of concealment, but also he had
become afflicted with unnatural jealousy, having realized that
he now had a rival for Mary's attention. No longer would
she passively obey his will when she had the boy on whom
to lavish her affection.

After the first shock the child suddenly found his voice; he screamed at the uncle, told him to turn the cart, and take him back home to his mammy.

" I don't want to go with you any more," he whimpered.

" It's no longer a question of what you want, ye wee bastard ! What ye need is a bit o' discipline; and I'm the one that'll teach it to ye ! " Having said this Welsh gave the child another blow that knocked him into the back of the cart with his nose bleeding profusely. There he lay and cried his heart out, until at last overcome by grief and weariness, he dropped asleep in the straw.

Most of us can remember incidents in our early lives; few of us could, I think, remember thoughts and feelings connected with those incidents. It is doubtful if many children of the age of six are in fact capable of an orderly sequence of thought leading to philosophical speculation. And how many of us can remember our childhood dreams ?

Thus when Hugh was to recount his experiences on the fearful nights of his journey to the Boyne home, he did so in such graphic form, and with such a wealth of detail that one is inclined to think that his inherent native ability as a story-teller may have inspired him to give his audience value for money, so causing him to draw on his vivid imagination. Albeit this is his own account of his dreams, thoughts, and feelings:

" As I lay asleep on the lightly straw-coloured boards of the cart I dreamed that a terrible monster was about to attack me; just at the moment when I thought I couldn't escape from the monster's teeth and claws my father appeared. He rescued me, and slew the monster. As I returned from the land of dreams to the reality of my situation, I kept calling for my father, but he wouldn't come to me."

" I can remember how the jolting of the cart pained my tender young body; and I was cold and damp. It was still dark when I awakened. As I looked upwards I saw the moon and the stars appearing and disappearing behind the menacing clouds of a watery sky. It all seemed to me at that moment so unfriendly and so frightening. Up to this I had looked on the moon, the stars, and the night sky as a comforting friend—now they seemed to be my enemies."

" I hate them ! I hate them ! I hate them ! This is how I felt when I watched the two figures on the seat in front of me. Even Aunt Mary, whom I regarded as my protector for a time, now seemed to be in league with this fiend of an uncle. I felt without a friend in the world. I wanted to die."

" Then I suddenly thought of prayer. My mother had always taught me to say my prayers before going to sleep: she told me to pray for all of them: my mother and father, sisters and brothers, and also for myself that God would protect me from all the difficulties and dangers of the world. Maybe it was because I had forgotten to pray that I now found myself in this terrible situation."

" As so I prayed, as many other children and adults for that matter, pray when they find themselves lost in an unsympathetic world. For a time I felt my case to be hopeless. There was nothing, nobody, up there in the night sky. I might as well reconcile myself to the fact that beyond my home and my mother's arms there was no power to protect me from the harsh world. With the thought of my mother in my mind my faith in ultimate goodness once again returned. I fell asleep."

Most of us have some memory of the joy we feel when we see the dawn come up after an uncomfortable and mainly sleepless night. Every dawn is a spring, a renewal of life and hope. This is how it is, or ought to be, in normal circumstances; but when circumstances are abnormal, there may come all too quickly a sudden realization of our predicament. Even then, at least when we are young, we feel that what seemed intolerable during the night has now become bearable—with renewed energy we may be able to do something about it. Stone walls no longer make a prison, nor iron bars a cage. With youth and strength in our loins we may be able to break down the walls and tear aside the bars.

So even wee Hugh, small, weak and defenceless as he was, when he awakened to find the sun warming his face, and gilding the heath-filled bogs and mountains around him, felt better. Imaginative children, and Hugh certainly belonged to this category, are sensitive to natural surroundings. As he sat up he saw away to the right the sun glinting the silver sea, and extending its great arc of light into the dew-filled foot-hills, and up through the rock and scrub of the mystical mountains of Ireland.

But his sense of beauty was suddenly quashed when he heard a rough voice saying:

" Here, take a drop o' this; it'll do ye good an' keep ye quiet for a while longer."

Thereupon a bottle of whiskey, from which Welsh and his wife had been taking occasional slugs, was thrust into the unwilling child's mouth. He coughed and spluttered as a gulp of the fiery liquid entered his throat. There were, no doubt, remonstrances from Mary, who was unlikely to have approved of giving such forceful treatment to a young child. Her remonstrances may not have been very strong, as in those days the giving of strong spirits to young children was not quite as unusual as it would be in our time.

The whiskey appeared to make the two in front more quarrelsome. According to Hugh's story they "fought the piece out" over the fifty pounds to be paid for the boy's keep, Welsh insisting that Mary must persuade her brother to pay fifty each year. If she didn't he would murder the pair of them; and leave them at the roadside.

On the other hand, as one might have expected, the spirit had an anæsthetizing effect on the youngster, enabling him to endure the cold, and the ever-present jogging of the springless cart on the pot-holed road. So with thoughts of his dear mammy on his mind, and the sound of bird-song in his ears, once again he sank into sweet oblivion.

Awakening for the second time he was warm at last; for now the sun had coursed up toward the zenith; and he could feel the wonderful life-giving rays permeating his whole body.

Suddenly he knew himself to be alone. There was no horse in the tilted cart. Freedom from discomfort now gave place to fear of desertion. There are circumstances when people would be glad to see another human face, even that of one of their worst enemies. Such was Hugh's plight at this moment that he would have welcomed the presence of those whom he had hated the night before. At least they represented some form of human contact in his immediate contactless world. But there was some reassurance in the sight of his aunt's highly coloured shawl which was spread over him when he awakened. If she had been going to desert him she wouldn't have left the shawl behind.

Looking around him he saw a thatched-cottage grocer's shop and public-house—a country spirit grocer's of the type to be seen all over the Irish countryside; there are many still in existence. What could have been more attractive to a young and hungry child than a little small-paned window, behind which were crusty loaves of bread, rosy apples, and bottles containing attractively coloured liquids.

" Neum ! neum ! " he exclaimed to himself. " What wouldn't I give to be behind that window ? " With his mouth watering he tried to clamber down from the cart; being unable to do so, he was assisted by a kindly blacksmith whose smithy stood opposite. He was just about to blurt out to the blacksmith the full story of his wrongs when his aunt, seeing him as she came out of the shop, quickly crossed to the other side, grabbed him by the arm, gently led him out of earshot, and into the shop where he was given potatoes and buttermilk, and allowed to lie on a settle-bed in front of the great turf fire. Before going asleep his aunt, with nerves on edge as to the possible consequences if he disobeyed, said with sincerity in her voice:

" Don't you ever attempt to speak to anybody ! Don't tell a single soul about what has happened to you ! If you do God help the two of us ! "

Already becoming inured to severity, he was not unduly disturbed. Here at least were food, warmth, and comfort. This was bliss. He fell asleep for the third time.

"Get up to hell out o' that wi' ye, ye lazy wee brat! 'Tis sleepin' all day ye'd be if somebody didn't take ye in hand!"

Again he was rudely awakened out of dreams of mother and home, and ordered to get up on the cart once more. Before he did so his aunt, partly out of kindness and partly so that he wouldn't appear to the public view with bloodstains on his face, gave him a bit of a clean-up with her damp handkerchief. While doing so she presented him with a bap and allowed him |to buy apples with his *hansel,* the few luck-pennies placed in the pocket of his new suit. Later he was to say that "it was ten years before I fingered another penny that I could call my own."

And so it went on: four days and nights in all, usually travelling by night in order, it would appear, to prevent the young fellow from chattering too much. During the day they rested at inns where the boy spent most of the daylight hours covered up and asleep in corners between the jamb-wall and the fire. His diet consisted mainly of bread and milk, or potatoes and buttermilk; these combined with his small store of apples probably supplied all that his growing frame required.

But the nights were terrible. "There was I," he would recount afterwards, "lying cold, damp, and stiff on damp straw, while the cart splashed and rumbled over pool-filled roads, and the rain poured down incessantly. At one of the inns my warm woollen suit was changed for an over-large suit of stiff corduroy; I could hardly bend in it. Over the top o' me they flung an old horse-cover; between the smell o' this and the smell o' the corduroy, I was near asphyxiated."

"At one o' the inns I managed to slip between the drinkers like an eel in a bog, till I was able to pluck the coat-tails of the busy inn-keeper."

" What is it yer wantin' ? " said the man as he looked down at me with a friendly grin on his face. " If 'tis a drink sure I've no drink suitable for a nipper o' your size. Away back into the corner there an' I'll give ye a drop o' milk when 'tis less busy I am."

" No, no ! I don't want milk; I want me mammy, they're takin' me away from her an' I don't want to go; I want to go home. Help me ! Please, sir, help me ! "

But the man, though he liked the boy, wasn't very bright. He didn't understand the child's almost baby-like prattle, nor could Hugh understand his brogue. Anyhow an innkeeper would have been very loth to interfere with the private affairs of the gypsy-like looking man and woman who appeared to be in charge of the boy.

" Well, ye see, it's like this like, I don't know what yer saying like, run along now back to them as is in charge o' ye like; an' mebbe I'll see ye later like."

Having said all he had to say, which was punctuated after every few words with *like*, the innkeeper took a long draught of his own brew. He had just turned toward one of his customers with the request:

" Now Pat, what can Ah give ye like ? "
when he heard an angry voice shouting in a kind of suppressed fury:

" Ye blasted wee spalpeen, Ah'll bate the guts out o' ye when Ah get ye out o' here ! Didn't Ah tell ye ye weren't to leave your corner on any account ? "

Poor Hughie, already half in tears because of the refusal of the innkeeper to help him, could contain himself no longer. He wept copiously, feeling that this new world into which he had been so rudely thrust, was indeed a lonely and friendless place. Though a few of those in the inn glanced at him curiously, as usual they passed by on the other side, not wishing to become involved in what appeared to be parental difficulty with a fractious and wilful child.

Soon they were on the road again. In spite of everything, when the sun showed itself Hugh could feel it's radiance penetrating his consciousness. He was always aware of the varied and often weird beauty of the countryside: the mountains, the hills, the woods, the streams, and gurgling water-filled rills, and the occasional glimpses of the eternally rolling sea. All these things so penetrated his young mind that the memory of them made an unforgettable impact; thus he was able vividly to recall them with power and drama, even when time caught up with the drama of his own life.

A hundred and twenty miles or so ! It was a long journey for a small boy cooped up in an uncomfortable, springless cart. Most children nowadays would become difficult enough on a similar journey in a modern car, complete with hydraulic suspension springs, and every other possible aid to bodily comfort. And when you add to the boy's physical discomfort his fear of his foster-father, and the torture of homesickness, you wonder how he survived. But survive he did, and as future events were to show, the experience, traumatic as it was, instead of destroying him, appeared to so toughen the fibre of his being that he was able that much better to endure all that was to follow.

That all good things come to an end is almost axiomatic; that all bad things come to an end is equally true. Hugh had now come to the end of his bad journey; but he had many a rough road to travel before reaching his journey's end.

CHAPTER 7

BLEAK DAYS AND BLACK NIGHTS

DROGHEDA at last, and then home—but what a home !
Anything more miserable could scarcely be imagined.
The house, the wonderful home that Hugh had been led to
believe in, was no more than a burnt-out shell roofed tempor-
arily with anything that could be thrown over it. Save for
the turf fire burning in the wide hearth, it was without comfort
of any description. But for the boy, stiff, cold, and bruised,
anything was a relief from the rumbling, jolting farm cart;
and he thought with joy of lying down anywhere, in any
rag-filled, or straw-filled, corner as long as it was quiet and
unmoving.

"God be wi' ye !" said a voice from the corner beside
the fire as they entered, "welcome home, sure 'tis the holy
saints themselves must 'a protected ye on yer journey. Faith
it's glad I am to see yez back in the ancestral home; the ould
place hasn't been the same since yez left."

But Welsh wasn't impressed. "Get yourself up to hell
out o' that !" he said. "I suppose ye've been sittin' on yer
arse there ever since. Put the kettle on for a drop o' hot
punch for the missus and meself. We're near starved wi' the
cowld and the wet; and put on a drop o' stirabout for the
young fella."

The big, lank, raw-boned, black-haired, sunken-cheeked
man rose up from beside the fire. As he was shuffling about
doing as he was bid, he said to Hugh:

"Ah sure now 'tis the darlin' boy ye are, may the holy
angels always look after ye. An' now, if I may ask, what
might be yer name ? Hugh, is it ? A Protestant name no

less; but we'll not let that stand agin ye if yer a good boy an'
do as yer bid. Let's have a look at ye! Ye've the makin's o'
a good bit o' bone an muscle there; it'll be no time till we have
ye doin' a man's work about the place."

"Aye, we'll make him work all right, Gallagher, an' no
nonsense about it. His father, the son of a bitch, gave me only
a fiver instead of fifty for his education and upkeep; the only
education he'll get will be in the fields. From now on,
Gallagher, he'll be your responsibility. Make him earn his
keep I tell ye, or there'll be no keep for either o' ye."

"Ah sure Mr. Welsh, that was a terrible trick for his father
to play on ye. May the Blessed Virgin and all the saints blast
him to hell for ever. You leave the lad to me Mr. Welsh;
I'll soon lick him into shape."

Hugh, having been released by Welsh who had been
gripping him by the shoulders in a vice-like grip, now had a
moment in which to look around at his new home. He was
surprised to see hens hopping in and out through the open
door; this was no unusual sight in an Irish farmhouse
kitchen; but he was shocked to find them doing this with
complete immunity. At his own home there would have
been an immediate shoo! shoo! out hens! and with a
great fluttering and squawking the intruding birds would
have been driven out to their own territory in the cobbled
yard. Here, however, nobody showed the slightest concern.
Not only did the hens and other domestic birds do this, but
also the dirty ill-kept pigs seemed to be allowed to snort and
root around the flagged kitchen without interference. Indeed
in one corner of the room a motherly, menacing-looking sow
kept watch and ward over her brood of piglets.

All the remaining Brontë belongings appeared to be
concentrated within this area. Furniture? there was precious
little of it. One or two chairs of a sort—used chiefly as hen
roosts—were upholstered with twisted straw. At the far end
of the room, away from the fire, was the bedroom, or more
correctly room for the bed, which consisted of a large four-

poster with decapitated legs. The blankets appeared to be mainly old sacks sewn together.

Comfortless and cheerless as the place was, it at least represented for the boy an improvement on the nightmare of the previous four nights. Albeit he couldn't believe that this was to be his biding place throughout the years to follow, so at last he said timidly:

" Are we going home soon, Uncle Welsh ? "

" Going home ! Going home ! Where the hell do ye think ye are ? This is the only home you'll ever know my lad; and if it hadn't been for me, ye'd never have been here. Ye'd have been kicked out by that father o' yours sooner or later. Yer here now an' it's here yer goin' to stay for the rest o' yer life, so you may as well settle down an' make the best o' it. I don't want any nonsense. The trouble wi' you is that yer a bit too big for yer boots. Away off to yer bed now, for ye'll have to be ready for a good hard day's work to-morrow."

There was, however, little rest for a weary boy. What with grunting pigs, pre-dawn crowing cocks, clucking hens, and the fact that, positioned badly, he had to lie at the foot of his aunt and uncle in a damp uncomfortable bed, he didn't sleep well; and when he awakened he felt so ill that he scarcely knew where he was or what was happening to him.

Welsh was up at cock-crow—or when the cocks should have been crowing if they hadn't anticipated the dawn—was soon out and about, not to feed the hens and pigs, but to make sure that both sets of animals would find as much of their own food as possible. Not only did he chase the pigs and poultry; but he also jerked young Hugh to feet on which he could barely stand. It was only when the boy collapsed completely that it began to dawn on Welsh that something was seriously wrong.

The inevitable had happened, the boy had contracted what would then have been described as *the fever*—typhoid, no doubt, from all the dirty milk, dirty water, and dirty food he had eaten on the journey. For weeks he lay in delirium, during which he was back in the arms of his beloved mother—at least one hopes that such delusions were with him to help him through the dark tunnel of disease and despair. There was no kindly country doctor to cheer him by day; nor night nurse to cheer him by night. As was the custom in those days they shaved off his hair; when he did recover he was as bald as a coot. Otherwise his treatment consisted of all the old-fashioned remedies largely administered by his Aunt Mary.

How Welsh regarded him at this stage we don't know—probably with surly silence, and with less concern than if one of his animals were dying. Aunt Mary, on the other hand, rose to the occasion; she proved to be a natural nurse who knew by instinct what was the right thing to do. When he was teetering on that borderland where life is on one side and death on the other, she, by her gentle coaxing kept him from drifting over to the wrong side of the border. And when nourishment would pass his frail lips she would give him just that little vital fuel, in the form of milk posset, to keep the flickering flame of life burning.

Death didn't cheat him, as he might have thought when at one time he wanted to die, but it *was* kept at bay by his Aunt's ministrations. Like many another woman who did the wrong thing at the wrong time, she rose to heights almost of saintliness at the right time. As Hugh began to recover, her affection for him became so strong that for many years it was to be the mainstay of her otherwise miserable existence.

Those of us who have had some form of childhood illness—that is most of us—will probably recollect that quite extraordinary sudden jump from illness to health: one day we still feel ill, weak, and helpless; and the next we are suddenly aware; we hear the clattering sound of dishes in the kitchen, and we know that loving hands will soon give us appetizing food, for which at last we have an appetite; if we read we ask for our favourite books; if we paint we ask for our paint-box; if we like to play with toy soldiers we ask for our toy soldiers. But for Hugh there were none of these: it was enough for him to become aware of the sun seeking chinks through the unglazed windows, or of the sound of the crowing cocks, the clucking hens, and the grunting pigs. And above all there was the shaggy mongrel Keeper which had taken such a fancy to the wee fellow that he rarely left his bedside throughout his long illness.

Toys are, after all, a mere substitute for reality. I wonder do country children play as much and as long with toys as would their urban contemporaries. I doubt it; for when you have real, live, living things with which to play, substitutes are not so necessary. So it came about that Keeper became at once the boy's teddy bear, toy soldier, toy train and all the rest. On him he lavished all his affection and all his interest; and what is more his affection was returned: the two were to become inseparable.

Even the domestic birds became his friends and playthings; the hens that would eat the crumbs from his hands; the big flaming cock that crowed the world as if he owned it; and the wee bantam that tried to win the attention of the barnyard ladies by using gentler tones.

" And what would the bouchaleen like to-day ? " Aunt Mary would say as he began to recover more and more. " What about a nice fresh egg ? Don't say anything to anybody. I have one here under me shawl ? " Or in a more conspiratorial tone she would suggest that, when everybody was away in the afternoon, the two of them would enjoy a nice cup of peppermint tea. " Do you all the good in the world."

And it did him all the good in the world; in fact on one memorable day soon afterwards she said:

" Would ye like to get up for an hour or two ? "

Would he like to get up ? Of course nothing would please him better. Oh to be up ! to be able to use his young limbs; to feel the fresh air around him; to feel the sun glowing his cheeks. Would he like to get up ? Need she ask.

But when he got up how disappointed he was ! He was not as strong as he thought. His legs wobbled like rickety old chairs; and there was no strength in him. Indeed after an hour or two he was only too glad to be able to crawl back between his rough blankets once more.

But as each day passed the vital sap began to rise in him more and more, until there came a memorable day when he found he was able to walk the length of the boreen. Though he still felt a little weak, the smell of Ireland's green land aroused a joy in him which was almost painful. As he looked around and saw the fields, the woods, and the winging birds he thought that, when full strength returned, he could face almost anything—even his bullying uncle and the wheedling detested Gallagher.

A troubled woman needs a confidant, or a confidante; she must unload her mind to somebody, even to a small child. Thus it was that throughout the long days of illness and convalescence Mary came to tell Hugh more and more of all that had happened. She told him about the old happy Brontë home; she told him about the homecoming with the foundling child; the child whom she half-loved and half-despised. He became her playmate largely because she had to protect him from the brothers who hated him. This led her on to tell him about the impossible situation in which she found herself; the only way out was through a marriage which she had regretted ever since. Finally there was the dissolution of her loved family, followed by the erosion of the cattle business and the farm. When she came to the bit about the burning of the old home Hugh could contain himself no longer; he burst into tears; the original home as she described it was exactly what he had imagined. His only consolation was that the tyrannical brute, Welsh, was no Brontë, not even an Irishman. Even at this early stage in his life he made a resolve that, come what may, he would sooner or later break the bonds that now held him in the service of this unspeakable ruffian. In the meantime his one consolation and buffer was the genuine love shown to him by his Aunt Mary. He felt they were conspirators against a common enemy.

But the honeymoon-like period was soon to be over. As Mary's obvious affection for the boy increased, Welsh's hatred of him grew in like proportion. Thus, as soon as there was any sign that the lad was sufficiently strong to be of use, he said to him:

" I'm not keepin' you for nothin' any longer. Ever since ye came here ye've been nothin' but a trouble and an expense. Yer strong enough to make a start to-morrow nornin'. It'll do ye good anyhow."

So on the morrow Hugh was dragged out of bed at what seemed to him an unearthly hour, after his long period of late mornings and early nights. Had it not been for continued remonstrance and resistance from Mary he would have been forced into the fields much sooner.

" This mornin' ye'll work with Gallagher; after that ye'll be on her own."

As it was now into early summer, and the fickle Irish weather had taken a turn for the better, Hugh's initiation was not as bad is it might have been under more adverse circumstances. The sky was clear blue, without a single cloud to clothe its beauty. To attempt to describe the grass greenness would be to attempt the impossible; it was all that has given Ireland its fully justified emerald title; and, interspersed between the blades of grass there were those thousands of wild flowers such as one rarely sees in these days of fertilizers and weed-killers.

Hugh walked through the dew-soaked grass with joy in his heart until he saw Gallagher waiting for him.

" Ah sure now if it isn't young Hugh himself. Sure now all the holy angels and the blessed Mary must have been wi' ye to bring ye through the dark night o' sickness. Wasn't it I was prayin' for you the whole time."

But Hugh, with the sure instinct of a child, no more trusted him than he would have trusted Satan himself. As the ungainly creature attempted to put his arm around him, he immediately drew back. As he did so Gallagher caught him by the ear.

" Now, now," said the man, " yer not afraid of ould Patsy are ye ? There's nothin' *to . . . be . . . afraid . . . of.*" As he spoke he emphasized each word by giving Hugh's ear a more or less painful tweak.

" There's nothin' to be afraid of at all, at all—not if ye do as yer bid ! O' course if ye don't, Patsy knows how to make ye ! "

Gallagher's reputation around the country was that of a cruel unscrupulous monster. To begin with he was a sub-agent's hack. He would spy here, there, and everywhere collecting information to be used later by the sub-agent and the agent, to enable them to *convict* and *evict*. And, as if this weren't enough he, in association with the notorious Meg of the Mary Brontë marriage, was an illicit dealer in bastard babies. Such are not to be taken as representative of the people of the Boyne Valley; they were to be found everywhere at this time. The mere fact that the people distrusted and ultimately destroyed Gallagher and his like is an indication of their total rejection. What made Gallagher even more objectionable was his unctuous religiosity.

At this stage his main concern was to get the child well and truly under his thumb:

" Do ye see them cattle up there in the field beyond ? Up there, as fast as yer legs 'll carry ye; and drive them down without lettin' one o' them stray ! Away off with ye now ! " said he, emphasizing his order by giving Hugh a boot on the backside to help him on his way.

" An may God go wi' ye ! If there's one o' them bastes missin' when ye get down here Ah'll split ye ! "

Hugh ran up the hill with Keeper behind him. It was his first attempt, and of course the cattle scattered here, there, and everywhere. Try as he would he couldn't regain control. At last, discouraged and crestfallen, he returned to Gallagher for help. The man knew perfectly well what would happen. When Hugh returned he was given a cuff on the ear; he was told that he was an ill-begotten son of a bitch; and that if he didn't mend his ways pretty quickly he would be damned to hell for ever !

As time wore on, however, Hugh became both stronger and shrewder. Soon he was able to control the cattle as well as any man; and he also learned to keep out of eyeshot and earshot of Gallagher on every possible occasion and in every possible way. He actually began to enjoy himself and the work. As his energy came to pile up in excess of what he needed, the sheer explosion of it, when he had to race this way and that after the animals, gave him as much joy as many a boy would find in a game of football or hurley.

Most of us would think that the conditions of his life were intolerable. This is how it would seem to those of us brought up in a more civilized way. One must remember that a young boy who is tired enough, can sleep almost anywhere and under any circumstances. There are few without youthful memories of nights spent in bell-tents, barns, or even on bare boards, yet even with opening heavens overhead, tired young bodies could pass into oblivion with an ease unknown in life's later years. So it was with Hugh: after the long day's toil he could have slept in a roadside ditch.

Health and strength probably depend more on diet than on any other factor. Hugh's diet was rough stuff compared with what many modern children might expect; for him there were no delectable dainties to tempt an appetite that never required tempting; there were neither grapes nor grape fruits, oranges nor aubergines, sweets nor sweet cakes. But there were porridge and potatoes, milk and buttermilk, possibly occasional pieces from a snared rabbit, or a shot hare, mush-rooms cooked by Mary on the turf top as a special treat, and maybe pieces of poached fish from the river. No doubt, too, he often gnawed a turnip from the field, or bit into a hard apple picked up in a brambley orchard, or he may have filled the empty corners of his belly with those luscious blackberries that grow as large and as freely in the hedges of Ireland as black grapes in Southern France.

Maybe his diet was spasmodic, maybe he was rarely able to eat his fill; but at least, if my surmises are correct, it was food with which the most expert dietician could scarcely find fault. And it was food which would help a growing boy to grow in body and brain, muscle and manliness.

As time was to show, he grew in all of these, though he had to survive a long period of fear of Welsh, and hatred of Gallagher, whom he despised. To some extent he also feared Gallagher because he knew that everything he did would be reported to headquarters; and if anything went wrong, the blame would be placed unfairly and squarely on his shoulders.

If, for example, cattle broke through into the small patch of sown land, Gallagher would probably give his own fallacious account to Welsh:

" Och, sir, now, as sure as me name's Gallagher; an' may I be struck down by the Almighty if I'm not tellin' the truth; an' it's not for me to get a young fellow into trouble, but 'tis mighty careless he's growin'. Wasn't it I that tould him to shut the gate into the corn field ? Divil the bit o' him done it; and what do ye think has happened ? The whole place is ploughed up an' it'll have to be re-sown."

" Do ye tell me that now, Patsy ? Send the young whelp to me till I bate a bit o' sense intil him ! "

" Ah, sir, 'tis yerself is a merciful dacent man; but as sure as God's me witness, I have to tell ye that he's gettin' worse every day; an' if ye don't scare the daylights out o' him he'll have us ruined."

The poor lad was called in; it was useless for him to deny the charge, though he knew full well that it was Gallagher himself who had left the gate open. In spite of Mary's protestations he was thoroughly beaten, and sent supperless to bed.

All this might have destroyed the spirit of a less spirited boy, but he was a Brontë and proud of it. Often as he watched and tended the scattered cattle, he thought that some day he would break the shackles, win his way to freedom, and maybe return to re-build the old house and the Brontë fortunes. Indeed the ruins were to become his retreat and resting place whenever retreat and rest were possible; and it was usually within the shelter of the crumbling walls that he dreamed those long, long thoughts of youth.

Though we don't know much about his life from childhood to adolescence and early manhood, we can make certain deductions in the light of future events. He must have grown as strong as any other man of his age and time. Doubtless he learned to ride in the hard way: by catching a horse in the field, springing on to his back, and riding him saddleless—and bridleless maybe—to the place required for Welsh to mount in a more dignified way. He probably learned to catch fish with a hazel rod and a horse hair, or perhaps by the now almost legendary method of *tickling*. That he learned to swim is certain—how? As he was certainly not taught by Gallagher or Welsh one can only conclude that he taught himself. What could have been more natural than for him to have removed his ragged clothes on a hot summer evening; then, slipping into the refreshing sandy shallows, he would have essayed further and further, until one day he found himself floating and becoming mobile with the movement of his young arms and legs.

He also probably became handy at the making of ditches, fences, and walls, and there wasn't a country lad living at the time who wouldn't have learned how to milk a cow and help a cow at the calving. It is likely that the drying and shelling of oats over a slow burning fire were practised in this part of the country; whether he took part in it or not he would certainly have seen the process in action, and his observations would have registered in his accessible mind.

All these skills and arts were to become of immeasurable value to him in the years to come.

When grown too big to sleep at the foot of the family bed he was relegated to a draughty, damp, partially roofless loft. There he slept on a straw-filled sack; there he continued to have dreams of home, and he would often awaken at night calling for his mama and papa, his sisters and brothers. At what stage do such childish memories become obliterated? One wonders if they are *ever* obliterated. Some psychologists maintain that the tendency to revert to childhood is omnipresent in all of us; and it is certain that many people consciously long to go back to the time when they prattled at their mother's apron strings. For Hugh every stranger he saw passing on his legitimate business along the Boyne-flanked road was a potential saviour; one who would rescue him from this dreadful place and carry him back to his home, his family, and his friends.

There are nights when our dreams are so pleasant that we would like to prolong the night indefinitely; there are others when dreams are so terrifying that we long for the night to end. We find it difficult to explain the difference. Not wishing to probe too deeply into causes, we generally dismiss the whole matter with the usual: too much cheese last night; too much beer; too late and too big a supper; any explanation in fact rather than look for the psychological cause.

In Hugh's case the cause was obvious, especially when he came under the influence of the man Gallagher. He terrified the lad both consciously and unconsciously: consciously by telling him stories deliberately designed to frighten; and unconsciously by telling him stories and describing events quite unsuitable for the ears of a young child.

"Did iver Ah tell ye about the night Ah was taking a short-cut through the glen up there?" he would say. "Ah hadn't gone very far when Ah saw a black-clothed figure in front o' me. His eyes were blazing with fiendish fires like two glowin' coals; and there were horns stickin' upwards from his head. 'May all the holy saints and angels protect me!' Ah said, ''tis the divil himself.' He turned toward me; he gripped me be the shoulders; and he told me that he'd tear the soul out o' me body. Then Ah bethought me to make the sign o' the cross: suddenly the divil let go o' me an' with a scream he disappeared into the night."

There were many similar tales of ghosts and goblins, fiends and fairies.

" Them fairies," he would say, " ye'd need to watch out for them, specially a bouchaleen like you. They'd take ye as fast as they'd look at ye—an' if iver ye came back—an' there's no knowin' ye would—ye'd niver be the same agin: ye'd niver grow up to be a man. It's the truth Ah'm tellin' ye, so God help me ! "

And so it went on: tales of headless horsemen, of ghostly appearances in haunted churchyards, of strange lights, and cries and screams. Is it any wonder the poor lad would sometimes awaken in his dark, rat-infested loft, after being shaken and terrified by a maddening nightmare or devilish dream ? In those days of course it wasn't unusual for children to be stuffed with such stories by unthinking servants, and even by parents with little psychological sense. And there were many bully-boys who deliberately set themselves out to frighten their listeners; the greater the effect the more they enjoyed themselves.

Somebody to talk to—somebody to talk to—that's what he needed; and he met few others to whom he could talk except the hated and despised Gallagher, who could have wheedled confessions from a covenanter.

" An' what were ye doin' last night over there behind the walls o' the ould house ? Sure 'twas meself that saw ye sittin' there all yer lone ? What were ye up to at all, at all ? "

With this opening gambit Gallagher hoped to draw the boy out; he was not disappointed.

" I was thinkin' about all me Aunt Mary told me," replied Hugh, " about how the house used to belong to my family; then Uncle Welsh came along; an' he stole it from my Papa and his brothers and sisters, an'—an' people didn't like Uncle Welsh, so they burned the house down. I hate Uncle Welsh, he's a bad wicked man ! "

" Ah, God forgive ye for sayin' such a terrible thing. 'Tis a mortial sin to hate anybody. If ye keep on sayin' the likes o' that ye'll have a terrible purgatory when ye die. Maybe 'twas yer father was the bad man for sendin' ye away."

" No ! No ! " Hugh said vehemently, " my Papa is not a bad man. He thought he was sending me to a good home. It's not a good home an' I'm going to run away when I'm big enough."

The conversation was duly reported to Welsh. Mary received a battering and Hugh a whipping. When it was all over Welsh said: " That'll teach ye a bit o' gratitude for all I've done for ye."

Gratitude ! Gratitude for what ? For cold, for damp, for deprivation, for constant scolding and whippings ? When eggs had disappeared, who had taken them ? Hugh, of course; when an animal went sick Hugh had neglected it. Every time these things happened Hugh got a beating; a less spirited boy would have been spirit broken.

At last he found another friend and confidant.

CHAPTER 8

THE RUNAWAY

ONE day, as he was working down near a piece of bogland which separated Welsh's farm from his nearest neighbour, a man hailed him from the other side.

" Hello there ! " said the neighbour.

" Hello ! " shouted Hugh with manifest delight at being greeted by another human being.

" 'Tis a grand day for sure," cried the man in a high-pitched voice as though he were speaking into a wind.

" Aye," replied Hugh, " 'tis a grand day."

" You're the Brontë boy; Ah've heard it said around the village that you're a good lad, but not gettin' the best o' treatment beyond."

" Ah try to do me best, but everything Ah do is wrong. They're all agin me except me Aunt Mary."

" Well ye've one other friend there: the dog, Ah see—a good hard workin' mongrel be the looks o' him. What's his name ? Keeper ! Here Keeper ! Keeper ! good dog, good dog."

At first the dog was a little suspicious, then realizing the man was a friend, he ran across, smelt him, and nuzzled against his legs.

A man who befriends my dog is my friend, thought Hugh; and indeed this was to be the beginning of a companionship with far-reaching consequences. To have some trustworthy person in whom to confide was to make Hugh's almost unendurable life durable. And the *rapport* between the two didn't end in mere sentiment; for the neighbour, realizing that most boys are always hungry, knew that Hugh

72

was hungrier than most. So a hard-boiled egg or two, a piece of home-baked cake, a mug of sweet milk, and other country delectables would often find their way from the bog's edge to the lad's stomach.

Strips of unused—and often unusable—land in Ireland have, from time immemorial, been the cause of bitter family and personal fueds between contending owners, or tenants; this particular strip was no exception. Time and time again, Welsh finding this man down on this piece of useless bog, would attempt to drive him away with abuse; and if this failed, even with stones, sticks, or staves.

The bog, not a bog in the best sense, for there was no turf on it, was covered with more or less tasteless star-grass; the hay from it would scarcely have kept a goat alive let alone an out-wintering steer; it was, in fact, useless for anything other than a bite of roughage, or bedding for indoor beasts. For all that its possession was a matter of bitter controversy.

Welsh tried to use his old methods of chicanery, bribery, and corruption. Before the assassination of the old agent, however, all his dealings and double-dealings had failed to bring about the desired result. The new man, wishing to keep a foot in both camps, proved to be a more difficult proposition, for he wasn't averse to receiving money from the two contending parties.

Finally things came to a head one day when the two men concerned were trying their hardest to recover the lion's share of the star-grass. As both of them, you might say, were " up to the oxters " in bog water, the conditions for a stand-up fight were not exactly favourable for either party. As it happened young Hugh, standing by to tie up the bundles and throw them on to the dry ground, was a witness to the proceedings.

" Get to hell out of it ! " shouted Welsh. " If ye don't Ah'll cleave ye with me sickle ! "

" Cleave away, Welsh ! " said the other calmly, " but if ye do ye'll swing from the nearest gallows-tree; an' there'll not be one around to shed a tear for ye, nor would there be

F

one to lift a han' to help ye; for there's not a man more hated in the whole townlan'."

"Holy Christ!" Welsh screamed, "just let me get at ye an' Ah'll rip the bowels out o' ye!"

Having said this he foolishly attempted to run forward; but as every sensible person knows, you can't run in water let alone in a bog; the result was that the man plunged head down into the filthy mire. Fortunately, for both him and the neighbour, he lost his sickle in the process. Before he could recover he received a blow on his prominent nose sufficient to turn that organ of his body in a different direction. He had scarcely recovered from this when what seemed like a blow from a sledge-hammer hit him hard between the eyes.

In the meantime Hugh, knowing that Welsh deserved every blow and more, made no attempt whatever to succour his uncle, even though the latter shouted at him to join the fray on his behalf. He knew what the consequences would be for him, but he was now strong enough and big enough to take his own independent line. Instead of supporting Welsh, he found himself shouting on behalf of his opponent. Two or three times he heard himself loudly exclaiming: "Hit him! hit him! smash him!"

In the end one final blow put Welsh on his back once more in the mud. Between them Hugh and Gallagher, who had appeared once the fight was over, dragged the bloody, muddy, bleeding man to firmer ground where he lay panting and breathing fiery imprecations at all of them. Eventually he struggled to his feet and staggered homewards, but not before telling Hugh that he would beat him within an inch of his life.

No sooner was he home than he repaired to his bed where he remained for some weeks. While he was there nobody counted save Welsh Brontë. His poor wife, with a twelve-months old baby to look after, was ordered hither and thither: she must bind his wounds, bathe his bruises, feed the brute, bath the baby, feed the hens, churn the milk, and altogether act as general factotum for the farm and family.

Whether or not the baby brought jubilation or despair is not recorded. Though it must have aroused Mary's latent maternal feelings, she could no doubt foresee complications. As for Hugh, few would expect a boy of sixteen to be particularly interested in babies, but the arrival of an heir of Welsh's own blood-line served to strengthen the boy's growing resolve to quit.

At fifteen he felt strong enough in body, mind, and will to stand up for himself, so when Welsh sent for him to upbraid him for his refusal to help in the fight, he found the tables turned:

" What did ye mean by it, ye bloody young disloyal turncoat. You that I brought from yer miserable home; you that I fed and clothed and reared. How dare you, ye young spalpeen ! You just wait 'till I'm out o' me bed o' pain and suffering—ouch ! " he exclaimed as though suddenly hit by a spasm of pain—" you just wait an' I'll give ye a hidin' that'll make ye wish ye'd never been born."

Hugh looked at him steadily, and emphasizing every word, he said:

" You did *not* give me a home ! You brought me to a house and farm stolen from my family, and then allowed to rot. You gave me a place to sleep in no better than you'd have given to one of your rotten cows. You never fed me properly, nor sent me to school. My father and mother would never have sent me here if they had known what things were really like. I love my Aunt Mary; but I hate you; and some day I'll get my own back. As for the fight, you knew perfectly well that the other man had at least as much right to cut the grass on the bog as you had. Why should I have helped you ? "

For once the normally sallow-faced man's skin reddened; and the veins seemed to stand out on his temples. An older man might have had a stroke. He almost rose out of the bed as he screamed:

" When I get out o' here, I'll flay the skin from yer body ! "

For Hugh the die was cast; if he had required any other brace for his resolve he had it now. He was not inspired entirely by fear; he would never again submit to the brutal indignity of a flogging by this man. The life of an individual is not just a steady, slow development; there are sudden leaps—sudden mental mutations. Yesterday we were stumbling over letters; to-day we can read; a few weeks ago we were small; to-day we have stretched—we are tall; the unsolved problem of the day before has become so clear in our minds to-day that we wonder what was the difficulty. Hugh was a trapped boy yesterday; to-day he had broken the bonds; he was a man with a man's strength of body and will. He now knew what he would do; he would leap over the wall.

How to do it: that was the problem. His clothes were in tatters; and what about food and money? When an opportunity presented itself he took the neighbour into his confidence. Could he help him?

"O' course Ah will," said he. "Now look here Ah'll tell ye what ye'll do. Let me know the day and the hour; an' I'll have a lock o' ould clothes stuffed into the river bank just below my place. Yer a good swimmer aren't ye? Take off them ould duds, dive into the water, and swim down with the current to a point that I'll mark wi' a stick an' a lump o' rag. They'll niver look for ye escapin' be wather. As soon as you get to the right place, climb quickly out keepin' low among the reeds; put on the clothes and away ye go along the hedges and ditches as fast as yer legs 'll carry ye; an' "—he said as an after-thought—" don't forget to look in yer pockets ye might find somethin' there."

Hugh thanked the man from a full heart. As the bandaged Welsh had been lumbering about the place the day before, he thought his beating was imminent; he would be down at the bog in the afternoon; and he would then let the neighbour know when he proposed making his escape.

When he reached home Welsh said:

"Yer for yer thrashin' to-morrow after ye bring the cattle home."

The same afternoon he met his friend at the bog for the last time. The two conspirators made final arrangements. When they had redd up around the house, he and Gallagher would be cutting thistles in the far meadow. At about ten o'clock or so Gallagher would send him up for the morning mouthful; Gallagher would never see him again, nor Welsh for that matter; he knew Welsh would be out of the house at the pre-ordained time.

If anything were needed to prove Welsh to be a vengeful sadistic fiend, it was the obvious leering satisfaction with which he brandished a specially cut hazel wand—facetiously described by him as his *tickler*—in front of the boy's eyes on the morning of the proposed beating. Had the man had a little more psychological sense he might have realized that the exhibition had little or no effect on Hugh: he showed neither fear nor interest. The only person who showed both was Mary who wept until her eyes became red with the weeping.

" Shut yer snivelling there, or I'll give ye somethin' to snivel about " was the only sympathy she received from her madman of a husband.

Even Keeper sensed trouble. Those of us who have been the owner of intelligent dogs know only too well a dog's extraordinary instinct for knowing what is in the minds of those around him: he will bark for joy when he knows joy is on the way; and he will become dejected and whine when he senses sorrow. Keeper was Hugh's problem that morning. For obvious reasons he couldn't take him; on the other hand leaving him was like cutting away a part of his soul. Having no alternative he was afraid that Keeper might attempt to follow him; so he had to take an acceptable risk: that the dog, not being very water-wise, would not plunge in after him.

By good luck the day broke fresh and fair. As soon as the cows had been milked, the byres mucked out, and all the cattle settled in their daily stations, equipped with their sickles Hugh and Gallagher made their way down to the grazed fields for the annual weed-cutting. Gallagher was, as usual, cruelly unctuous.

" God help ye ! May the Lord an' his holy angels protect and save ye ! The master up there's goin' to make ye howl for mercy; but always remember to treat him with love an' affection in the future; because, as ye'll soon find out, it's all goin' to be for yer own good. In a year or two ye'll be rememberin' him with gratitude in yer prayers. You take Patsy Gallagher's word for it: he's an older man nor you."

Hugh walked on maintaining a stubborn silence.

" That Pa and Ma o' yours; they were no good. If ye'd listened to me years ago things would have been different now. Wasn't it meself toul ye they'd never come near ye?— an' they didn't."

At last Hugh was stung into retort: " Would ye shut up, for God's sake, an' leave me Pa and Ma out of it. How were they to know I wasn't happy ? "

" Happy ! Happy ! Ye betther not say ye weren't happy or Welsh 'll give ye a few more strokes o' the stick to persuade ye otherwise. Now if ye were to say that ye'd never been happier in yer life than workin' here with Patsy Gallagher, maybe the saints might intervene, an' ease the strokes on yer back. Ye could also say that ye'd come to yer senses an' ye knew yer Ma and Pa were not as ye thought they were."

" Would ye shut yer blasted mouth ! " shouted Hugh, exasperated beyond measure, " or Ah'll not be responsible for what Ah'll do to ye ! "

Like all insensitive fools Gallagher blindly walked into what was coming to him.

" As for that Ma o' yours, Ah could tell ye a thing or two about her."

" Ah min' one summer evenin' when the birds were quit singin, the two o' us were left alone in the hay-field. Before Ah knew what was happenin' to me she had me down beside her on the hay. Though Ah called on the Blessed Virgin herself to protect me she'd take no refusal."

This was the last straw. Before Gallagher quite knew what was happening he was at the receiving end of two hammer blows, one in the face, and the other in the region of the solar plexus. Down he went in the thistles, so that his nether end collected as many thorns as its surface area could collect.

" By God ! " said he getting up, " if I don't have yer life for this Ah'll see that yer uncle does the deed for me."

As soon as he was on his feet Keeper, too, joined in the fray. While Gallagher's long-armed punches flew wide of their mark, Hugh dodged underneath with the agility of youth; every punch went home, most of them right into the man's face. At the same time Keeper had a hold of his trousers which he pulled with so much vigour that Gallagher was soon left without as much as a pair of pants to cover his nakedness,

Leaving him there blubbering among the thistles, Hugh, with unimpaired vitality, bounded over the fields; end rushed into the house where he threw his arms around tear-stained Aunt Mary and kissed her; having dutifully kissed the baby also, he was down to the river's edge in a trice. Once there he whipped off his rags, threw them into the river, and made the plunge that was to divide him for ever from the Boyne Valley house and its associated miseries.

CHAPTER 9

MOUNT PLEASANT

OH, that plunge into the clear, cool, waters of the Boyne! Would he ever forget it? It wasn't just the physical effect on his young body. It was a purification, a renewal, a sacrament, a baptism. Call it what you will, he suddenly felt that all the filth and miseries of his life since he was six years old, were caught up in the flood, and borne away from him for ever and ever. He could hear himself praying his first prayer of gratitude: " Thank God! thank God! thank God! "

But he had to keep his head; pursuit was a probability; it might be on the way already. With the current behind him, however, his long easy strokes soon carried him downstream to the appointed place. There it was as promised, the tiny rag flag floating in the westerly downstream wind. In Hugh's eyes no gaily coloured pennant could have spelled out a more joyful signal.

And there were the clothes in a hole in the bank: a suit—too big for him perhaps—but a suit for all that. And what was this? a pair of boots! A pair of boots by heavens! He hadn't had a pair of boots on his feet for years. When he put his hands in his pockets he was like a child with a Christmas stocking: money, and food—yes, food that should see him well on his way to freedom.

Freedom! freedom! freedom! He repeated the word over and over again. He identified it with the flowing water of the Boyne. He had often looked at it, and his imaginative poetic mind had symbolized it with the freedom of the high-ways and by-ways for which his young heart had longed for so many years. Why hadn't he done this long ago? He was too small, too weak, too young; he would have been like a fallen leaf, a waif on the highways of the world blown hither and thither without purpose or direction.

But now he was strong; he could be a man amongst men. He had fought his fight against tyranny and blackguardism. He knew he could stand with or against anyone. Things wouldn't just happen to him; he would happen to them. He could work and live on his own terms. Never again would any man hold him in subjection and subservience.

In the meantime two matters were of vital importance: he must put as much ground as possible between himself and his uncle; and he must find work. He knew he could live for days as a vagrant. When his small supply of food ran out, he could buy a little. He could eat berries, and turnips; he could even beg if necessary. But he couldn't live in such a way for very long; he might invite suspicion—that could be fatal. He didn't quite know to what lengths his uncle might go to get him back again: not very far, he thought, unless out of sheer venom or spite. None-the-less he would have to be careful, especially for the first day or two.

As he headed downstream, he had some regrets, not the least being his desertion of Keeper. Nobody knows exactly what goes on in the animal mind, but most of us who have kept dogs, and have been dog lovers, have seen that appealing look of sorrow and desolation in a dog's eyes when he realizes we are about to leave him. We are not told whether or not Mary was privy to the escape, but it seems pretty certain that she must have known what was afoot. Hugh remembered her tears and admonitions, and her last cry of " God go with you ! "

In any circumstances who could have blamed the boy for his action ? That he was afraid of Welsh and his threat of severe punishment is without question; none save a masochist would have been without fear in such circumstances. The fear of a bullying schoolmaster's birch has caused many a schoolboy truancy in the past; when caught it was always the boy, not the master, who was at fault. In spite of Welsh's infamous character, Hugh knew that if he were to be apprehended, the weight of authority would be on the side of authority.

Thus it was that as he sped along the road his mind was a confusion of regret, fear and joy, but above all joy. And there was that overpowering sense of adventure. It is sometimes said that animals built for speed enjoy the hunt as much as the hunter; this is a moot point; but certain it is that a boy's sense of adventure often finds satisfaction in being chased; indeed, sometimes minor acts of vandalism are committed for this very reason: the boys concerned are simply inviting their elders to chase them. When the writer was a boy such games as " Hounds and Hares " were very much in vogue. One such game, locally invented, was known as " *Jack, Jack, show your Light.*" Jack, the quarry, would set off with a flash lamp which he would flash from various points in the fields and woods; the hunters would race to this point only to find Jack's flash now proceeding from some quite different place. How well R. L. Stevenson knew the mind of a boy when he wrote *Treasure Island* and *Kidnapped.*

Hugh neither knew of nor needed such games; the game he was playing was much more serious. Nevertheless the possibility of pursuit certainly added spice to the whole adventure. Thus it was that as he hurried on his way, while there was a song in his heart, his head and ears were attuned to every sound. And there were many sounds: never before had he been so acutely aware of the music of running waters, the sound of song birds in the trees, the craik, craik, of corn-crakes in the meadows, and the lowing of cattle on lowland and hill-land. The distant clop, clop, clop of horses on the hard road was enough to make him jump for cover. At one stage the noise of a jaunting-car load of rowdy passengers made his fast-beating heart beat a little faster, especially as there was no available cover. But all went well except for a few taunting remarks about his somewhat bizarre tailoring.

Skirting Drogheda which, for obvious reasons, he had no wish to enter, he was soon on the rocky road to Dublin—

or in his case away from Dublin—and it wasn't rocky, quite the reverse, in fact, as it headed straight as the crow flies toward Dunleer. As every walker knows, fatigue can be in direct proportion to the straightness of the road; to have the miles ahead obscured by bends has such an illusory effect that one is far less conscious of the miles ahead. Also, Hugh felt on the long straight stretches that he was like a single tree in a bare field; he could be seen from miles back.

But he was not unduly worried by either fear or fatigue; and the miles slipped by under his sturdy young legs with an ease that surprised the man himself. Never had he felt more manly: the fight, the plunge into the cold river water, and the change of clothes had given him such a feeling of health and courage that he felt competent to journey to the ends of the earth if necessary. There is no place in Ireland without its songs, singers, whistlers, and fiddlers, and Hugh, in spite of his lack of liberty, had picked up a few tunes on occasional cattle-driving journeys to Drogheda fairs; and so, with his boots on his broad shoulders, his bare feet trod the grass verge lightly when accompanied by the ballads of Boyne.

With little to worry about now he covered the few Irish miles from Dunleer to the pretty castled village of Castle-bellingham at what seemed a remarkable speed. Here he paused for a while to rest, and eat a bite beneath the bridge across the densely wooded stream. As he lay there by the willow-margined, well-wooded bank he could watch brown trout rising as he had rarely seen them rise before. Like many another in similar circumstances, he longed for some sort of gear with which to catch the golden beauties.

But he must be on his way; and so to Dundalk with which he was not impressed: too many people around, too many shops and traders; and what could either have meant to him who had barely enough pence with which to buy a morsel of supper? He now decided to move eastwards through the hilly and beautiful lands between Dundalk Bay and Carlingford. Here, where rich Ravensdale runs down to the lovely lands of Ballymascanlon, he found a sweet-smelling hay rick in which to rest his road-weary limbs. He went asleep.

On awakening he found he was hungry. There are pubs in the neighbourhood; a few of them have remained as they must have been when Hugh purchased his bread and cheese maybe, and, possibly, beer; it would probably have been white, low, thatched and beamed. There is one at the little village of Grange; could this have been where he stopped ? Who knows ? It is certain that he was in the area for he was now heading down to the coast near Carlingford.

What a sight it must have been for a boy unaccustomed to mountains ! Here was Cahir Linn Fjord—or Carlingford—dividing the Cooley Mountains on his side from the massive Mournes on the other—a lovely sight at any time, but on a blue summer evening incomparable. Hugh didn't know then that for the remainder of his life the Ring of Mourne would always form a part of his skyline.

Soon he found the tiny walled town of Carlingford nestling under Slieve Foy. Feeling a little disconsolate now that fatigue was on him, and the inevitable reaction to his adventures had set in, he wandered along the coast and then inland for an hour or two. At last he saw his pillar of smoke. Smoke—fire: these have always attracted lonely travellers; Hugh was no exception: smoke spelled work, warmth, comfort; and so he headed for the source. It proved to be a lime works, at a place called Mount Pleasant.

Hie there you ! " said the foreman when he saw him. " Are ye lookin' a start ? " His accent and idiom indicated a Northerner.

" Indeed I am," said Hugh.

" Are ye a hard worker ? "

" Sure I've never known anything else."

" You're a likely enough lookin' lad; let's see ye swing thon hammer."

Hugh lifted the heavy sledge; tired as he was he easily swung it over his head, brought it down on a large piece of limestone, and smashed it into fragments.

" Soul an' ye'll do," said the foreman. " Report to me at seven o'clock in the mornin'. Ye'll get good wages for good work."

It was dry, clean and warm around the kiln. All he needed was a wisp of easily procurable hay to give him the most comfortable bed he had slept on for a decade; and oh, what a sleep he had ! It was only when the dawn glow came up out of the eastern sea that he stirred. Before long carts began to rumble up to the kiln; in no time he was hard at it: smashing, shovelling, wheeling, and filling the white lime carts that fanned in from all quarters. Builders and bricklayers, farmers, and farm hands; they were all there; but for the most part they were all in good heart and good temper. After all this was a day out, a meeting place; most of them were old friends and acquaintances—the crack was good.

Hugh was accepted as one of themselves without question. By now he was a handsome, reddish haired, and upstanding boy. To outward appearances anyhow; his earlier experiences had left no mark; rather had they strengthened his character; and made him more determined than ever to get all he could from life, living, and whatever leisure might come his way. In no time he was popular with his workmates and with the clients.

In spite of the fact that he could neither read nor write, or possibly because of it—he had a highly receptive mind; and he was soon to discover that he had quite a gift for words, and for dramatic description.

Often, as he and the other men sat around the fire having their mid-day *piece,* he would tell the tale of his terrible journey; and the one they loved to hear most of all was his account of the final settlement with Gallagher and his watery escape.

" Tell us thon 'un again, Hughie," they would say as their eyes crinkled, and they hugged themselves in anticipation of of the final *dénouement*.

" An' ye knocked the bugger on his back among the thistles ? God ! Ah'd love to have seen ye ! " a man said, as he rubbed his hands together like one who had seen his favourite players score a goal at a football match.

Some of the men were well versed in local lore and legend. They were able to tell Hugh about Finn MacCool; they even pointed out his grave there in the mountains.

" Man," one of them said, " he was that big he could a' stepped over Slieve Foy as aisy as ye'd step over a ditch. He near copped it one night when the big snow-fella—Rusky or somethin' the giant from Scotland—he it was that did the dirty on Finn; he stole his sword when he was asleep; but yer man got the better o' him; for he lifted the great stone—the Cloghmore—flung it across at him and bashed him."

" Did iver ye hear the one about the Queen o' Connaught ? 'Twas herself that tried to take Daire of Ulster's bull by force; she damn near succeeded but ould Cuchulainn fought the piece out with her at Faughart. Cuchulainn was killed, but when she got the bull home didn't he near gore the lot o' them. They had to let him go in the end; and he fought his way back 'till he found a good dhrop o' Ulster grass."

Then another told the story of the tall black-haired, beauty of Spain whose Irish husband had won her by rescuing her from pirates; but when she saw the wild land allotted to her husband in an Esau-like arrangement with his wily brother and father, she was so disappointed that she lay down and died. " An' thon's her grave over there at the back o' them hills; an' it's called ' The Long Woman's Grave " 'till this day."

All these stories served to fire Hugh's romantic imagination; the more so because he, with his untutored mind, believed them.

In spite of the hard toil, he was happy now with good money coming in week by week. Where did he live ? No one knows for he was silent about this. One can but assume that he found lodgings somewhere in the district; and, since he makes no mention of them, the lodgings must have been to his liking.

Was it chance, fate, or God that brought about a meeting and a friendship, which eventually led to the writing of the famous Brontë classics, and the hundreds of books about these books ? Only God knows the answer to this question.

One day a cart drew up at the kiln. Hugh at once took a liking to the man in charge: age about the same as his own, colouring of hair similar; and the young man's friendly, open, and generous countenance at once captured him.

" Where are you from ? " said Hugh.

" Where am Ah from ? " Ah'm from the County Down, over there on the other side of the Mournes—a grand country—ever been there ? "

" No," Hugh answered, " but Ah hope to travel that far one o' these days."

Noticing that Hugh had the more rounded accents of the South, the other said:

" And yourself, where are ye from ? "

" Did ye ever hear of a place called Drogheda at the mouth of the Boyne Water ? That's where I came from; an' please God Ah'll never be back."

"Why ? "

" Och, now, it's a long story; but Ah'm better off here; me home there wasn't very happy."

" Sure Ah'm sorry to hear that, man. As me mother often said: ' Ye never know what goes on behind closed doors.' Everybody has their trials and troubles; but Ah'm glad to say we all get along well over at Ballynaskeagh. Got a nice wee farm there—a few horses an' one thing an' another—always plenty o' work—but we have our good times too—dancin', fiddlin', an' singin'—game o' cards now and again—sometimes a bit o' horse racin'.—a good life. Grand stuff for the lan' this lime ! Well Ah must be off now—see ye nixt time."

Hugh looked after him wistfully. " Nice to have a bit o' fun," he thought. So far his life had all been hard work. But he had money in his pocket now; to date he had found little on which to spend it. He began to think of bright-eyed girls he had seen on occasional visits to Dundalk. Maybe a clean-up and a suit of clothes would be a good idea. In one of the shops he had seen a suit at a price he thought he could afford. He'd get a lift in on one of the carts returning on Saturday evening.

And he bought his suit; what a treat for a fellow who had never had a decent suit since he was six; now he was sixteen; just at an age when the normal young fellow begins to think more about his appearance. As he walked about in Dundalk he felt as well-dressed as the best of them. Now when he saw a pretty girl he was able to return glance for glance with confidence.

As time moved on he became more and more familiar with the customers at the lime works, especially those from Ballynaskeagh and Glascar; Todds, McAllisters and others; and the friendship with the red-haired Paddy McClory blossomed to such an extent that when Christmas was near, Paddy paused for a moment as they were heaving a load into the cart; he wiped his brow; and pushed his cap up on his forehead.

" Listen, Hugh," he said almost shyly. " Ah've been thinkin' ye wouldn't want to spend Christmas be yer lone. What about comin' along to our place ? Ye'd enjoy a bit o' a break: horses, huntin', and mebbe a barn dance or two. An' ye know Ah have a purty sister; she'd enjoy your company."

Hugh, who could hardly believe his ears, was so overcome with gratitude that he was almost speechless. When he did manage to find his voice he said:

" Oh, thank you, Ah . . . Ah . . ."

" Quit talkin', man," replied Paddy, " yer welcome ! "

CHAPTER 10

HAPPY CHRISTMAS

CONFIDENCE in Hugh's ability had grown to such an extent that he was appointed overseer. Not only was this a considerable boost to his ego, but it also gave him more money in his pocket at a time when he needed it most. With the proposed visit to Ballynaskeagh in view he would require more clothes; and he also had the good sense to realize that a Christmas guest must bring Christmas presents to his hosts.

Thus in the weeks preceding the season of good will, he was often to be seen in Dundalk of a Saturday evening making his purchases. As he had no woman to advise him there was a problem. There are those with a sure instinct for such matters; others less fortunately endowed, are completely lost amid the maze of toys and trumperies, perfumes and perquisites of every description. For one with so little experience Hugh managed remarkably well; being generous by nature, he had no cost complex; thus as long as his money lasted he continued to buy without stint.

There are countrymen who look like countrymen no matter what clothes they wear; there are others who fit into good clothes as though they had been born that way. Since Hugh, according to all reports, was strong, handsome, and extraordinarily confident considering his early upbringing, he looked the part of a country gentleman, rather than a masquerading countryman.

And so when, on Christmas Eve, he ordered a gig in Newry to take him to Ballynaskeagh near Glasgar, the driver accepted him as one who could pay his fare and would pay

89

handsomely. As he was driven along he noticed everything; his farming eye took in the possibilities of this rich farming land with its low drumlins and its tiny, sheltered good-grazing, good-cropping farms. He noticed that it was well fenced, well ditched, and well drained; and that the cattle appeared to be sleek and healthy. Looking back from the hilltop town of Rathfriland he could see the magnificent Mournes piled up in snow-capped winter splendour.

Below Rathfriland they swung right and then left again heading for Glasgar and Ballynaskeagh; they passed an old mill, crossed a little bridge, then turned right along a tiny glen; and there they were in the McClory hamlet near Emdale. When they drew up at the most pretentious cottage Hugh's heart began to beat a little faster. Meeting people for the first time can be an ordeal for many, but when you are just on the threshold of manhood; when you have never been a guest before; and when you know there is a pretty girl around, you are bound to feel a little nervous no matter how sure of yourself you might be in normal circumstances.

When the door—or half-door—opened; and when he saw the vision framed therein, the heart that had been beating faster almost ceased to beat. So confused was he that he almost forgot to pay the gig man; and when he recovered sufficiently he paid the man far too much.

" Hugh, isn't it ? " said the violet-eyed beauty.

" Ah am," our hero, feeling somewhat unheroic for the moment, replied.

" Come in and welcome, Hugh; I'm Alice."

Love at first sight ? Yes, you could call it that, if indeed there is any other kind of love. The cynic might argue that there is no such thing; that it is all a matter of circumstance, physical attraction and so forth; that if there is such a thing as love, it must be built up on the firmer basis of friendship, community of interests, and on the solid virtues of mutual respect. Rubbish ! No two young people come together on such terms: either the whole chemistry of being-body, soul, and spirit-suddenly come together in one moment of immediate attraction, or they never really know what love is about.

And so it was with these two: at their very first meeting there was that flash of insight which showed them that the whole future course of their lives must lie along the same composite intertwined paths, irrespective of whether the path would be as straight and smooth as a Roman road, or as rough and crooked as a mountainy loanin'.

Since there is no portrait of Alice in existence, the only picture we can have of her must be imaginary. She has been described as the prettiest girl in the County Down at the time; that speaks volumes, for Down girls are remarkable for their prettiness. She has also been described as a Celtic Irish beauty, whatever that may mean. But when we are told that her hair consisted of luminous gold ringlets, her forehead was Parian marble, and her hazel, violet-tinted eyes had long brown eyelashes, her teeth were regular lustrous pearls, and her cheeks were roses of health, is it any wonder that young Hugh was completely entranced when he saw her ?

" Come on on in," Alice said without embarrassment; she was obviously in complete command of the situation, while Hugh, on the other hand, felt a little oafish and awkward.

" My brother 'll be in presently. In the meantime could I give you something to drink: tea, milk, whiskey if you would like it ? " Knowing that tea was still a rare and costly commodity, and not being a whiskey drinker, he asked for a glass of milk. His request was immediately granted; Alice, with grace and a smile that put him at his ease, handed him a glass of delicious, fresh, creamy milk ladled from a spotless muslin-covered pail.

It would be completely unrealistic to state that Alice was quite unaware of her beauty, and of its effect on those of the opposite sex; in this respect she was a normal young girl of the type that has existed in all generations. But she was completely natural, unselfconscious, and free from coquetry. Unlike many other attractive girls, her approach to men was artless; she had no wish to make every young fellow declare himself to be her ardent admirer. Had she known it this very quality made her more attractive to most, especially in County Down where naturalness is a highly appreciated characteristic.

" Paddy has told me quite a lot about ye, Hugh. You and he seem to be very friendly," she said.

" Och, aye; right enough we're good friends. Ye see Paddy was mighty good to me when I started at the kiln. He introduced me to a lot of the customers, especially from around here—grand people too."

" It must be hard work at the kiln."

" It's hard work right enough; but sure what about it ! Ye might as well wear out as rust out. Ah like hard work in the open air. An' when ye've dacent people around ye, and good wages, that's the main thing."

" You're right there. Paddy tells me it wasn't always like that with you."

" It was not. Ah didn't know what it was to have a good home since Ah was six; an' Ah can hardly tell ye what it means to me to have been invited here for Christmas."

" Sure you're as welcome as the flowers in May, Hugh. Christmas wouldn't be Christmas without someone here. Make yourself completely at home. Paddy and I like to see people enjoying themselves."

" Oh, an' that reminds me, Ah brought ye a bit o' a present; it's not very much, but Ah think it'll suit ye . . ." He paused for a moment wondering whether he dare say it; at length he plucked up courage: " Ye've lovely hair."

It was out: something he'd been longing to say since his arrival.

For a moment Alice was confused; a lovely blush made her glowing cheeks glow more brightly. But the situation was saved when she heard the sound of a horse being pulled up in the yard.

MORRIS FERGUSON 1978

Magherally Old Church —where Hugh and Alice were married.

The Ballynaskeagh Brontë Home.

" There's Paddy ! " she said, half-relieved and half-disappointed that the *tête-à-tête* couldn't have been continued a little longer.

" God bless all here ! " was Paddy's hearty greeting as his red head appeared over the half-door. " Why if it isn't the man himself ! " With his two hands he caught Hugh's right, and wrung it until Hugh thought that even his strong bones would crack.

" Man Ah'm glad to see ye ! Welcome ! Welcome to Ballynaskeagh ! "

While the two young men were exchanging compliments and reminiscences, Alice busied herself about the kitchen. In the excitement of Hugh's arrival she had nearly forgotten it was Christmas Eve. There was a lot to be done about the place, and many preparations to be made for to-morrow's feasting. She must have as much as possible ready before going off to Midnight Mass.

Friends, friends, friends: they called in droves. Everybody was in great heart; and in even greater heart before leaving, for it was a good old Irish custom that each should have a noggin or a pint. For a time the wide fireside seemed scarcely wide enough as the diameter of the circle around it increased. Hugh was in his element, especially as, without turning his head, it was enough to sense Alice hovering in the background, busy at the wide dresser that took up the whole back wall. From time to time she would have to break the circle to reach the bubbling pots, or the ovens with their glowing turves above and below. When she did so there was always a measure of banter in which Hugh didn't join.

" If ye don't move back now it'll be yer own dinner ye'll be gettin to-morrow," Alice would say.

" Move back ! move back ! Och, sure Ah'll move back all right; but watch ye don't trip over me an' fall into me lap; for if ye did, min' ye, it mightn't be so aisy to move out o' it again."

But Alice was always ready:

" Och, now Johnnie, would ye quit coddin' me. Ye ought to be ashamed o' yourself; an' you with a wife and half a dozen bairns."

" Yer keepin' very quiet there, Hugh," another would say. " Man, Ah wish Ah was your age wi' a purty lass like Alice around the place."

" Ah' min' the time," the story-teller began, " Ah was talkin' to a man at a fair. He came from a place on the coast; now what was the name o' it—me memory's not what it used to be—Kil somethin' or other?"

" Kilkeel," somebody volunteered.

" Aye, dammit, Kilkeel, that was it for sure. Anyhow this man, he vouched for the story, because he said he knew the farmer concerned as well as he knew his own mother. Wan day the boyo, who did a bit o' fishin' as well, went down to the rocks to see how his nets was doin'; while he was sittin' there what do ye think comes out o' the wather but a mermaid; and man she was as good-lookin' as Alice herself here.

" Afther a while she takes off her fish's tail an' scales, an' she lays down beside him. Yer man was a bit cute like, an' while the lassie wasn't lookin' he whips away the fancy costume an' tucks it under his coat. Be this time he'd a quare armful of her; an' after a bit o' coortin' he asks her to come up home wi' him. He passed no remarks to nobody; an' he was very careful to hide the fish costume away up in the rafters o' the house, in a place he thought she'd never find it.

" Time went on, yer man was as happy as Larry, an' Ah'm tellin' no lies when Ah say they'd two o' the loveliest childer ye ever seen.

" One night when the boss was away fishin' or somethin' there was a terrible storm; and the mother goes up to see if everything was right about the rafters when, what do you think? She finds her costume. The next day she sets off early in the mornin' an' from that day to this the farmer never heard tell of her."

There were tales of leprechauns and fairies, and of course, ghost stories galore. The glen opposite appeared to be a favourite haunt for haunting ghosts, and for ghost hunting. One man told a story in such vivid and graphic detail that Hugh never forgot it; years later when he was the centre of the story-telling circle, this tale was to become one of his star turns. The man told his story as follows:

"Once on a time," said he, "there was a fella lived near here—a bad rip he was—a regular son o' Satan if ever there was one. He had been coortin' a wuman off an' on for some time; an' then one tarrible dark night he ast her to go into Rathfrilan' wi' him for to buy a ring—at least that's what he said. But the only ring she got was when he tried to wring her neck. She managed to escape, an' was makin' her way home to her ma along the lonies and ditches when this fella, seein' what she was about, headed her off in the Glen here.

"This time he wasn't to be foiled. He maltreated her down there in the depths and darkness of the Glen as no woman had ever been maltreated afore. But she got her own back in the end for one night her ghost appeared in his cabin; it dragged him from his bed, and amid screams that could be heard throughout the whole townlan', the ghost pulled him down and down into the bottomless pit o' hell. Her ghost still. . . ."

"Time for Mass now boys," a sweet voice said—sweeter to Hugh than to anyone. They were a mixed lot of course, of different persuasions. With a "see ye to-morrow boys" they scattered this way and that according to their own denominations and inclinations. Hugh had no inclination to go to Mass, or any other church for that matter. Though he knew his family to have been traditionally Protestant, he had never been instructed in any form of religion, Catholic or Protestant, and so he didn't wish to look and appear ignorant and awkward when he made his first visit to a church.

When they had all gone he was left alone with his thoughts—alone in the rushlight with the ghost-haunted Glen in front, and the occasional grunt from the cattle behind.

But if all the foul fiends or fairies, ghosts or goblins of the mysterious underworld of that countryside had appeared to Hugh, they wouldn't have turned a hair on him. He had but one thought in his mind—the thought of Alice. He knew now that whatever might happen to him in the future, he would never be quite the same man again. He knew that whatever happened in the future would be inextricably bound up with this lovely girl. If he had to fight for her, by God, he would fight for her.

It is all too easy to be cynical in these days of sex cynicism, when romance has been reduced to its lowest common denominator. But try to remember " When you and I were seventeen "; and also try to remember that up to the age of seventeen this boy had been completely cut off from the companionship—or even acquaintance with—a girl of his own age; and then suddenly he found himself in close proximity to one who appeared to have all the attributes of a girl of his dreams. In such circumstances is it any wonder that Alice became his overriding obsession ?

Before the return from church Hugh had taken his thoughts with him to bed. Enough was enough for one day; it had been a long day for him: an early start, and then the long jogging journey through the roughly-roaded countryside on roughly sprung vehicles. Though he had enjoyed it all, he didn't wish to trespass too much on his hosts' time; he knew that they also would be tired and ready for a good sleep before to-morrow's festivities.

When he did go to bed in the low-raftered room, it was a long time before his eyelids closed; his mind was so occupied and preoccupied with the day's events. In most novels it is usual to state that love-possessed sleepers immediately begin to dream that they are defending the object of their love against a ruthless rival, or against some primitive brutish beast. How are we to know what anyone dreams about if they are unwilling to tell us ? In this case Hugh didn't tell anybody about his dreams; and in fact we think he didn't dream at all from the time his eyes closed until he heard the familiar farmyard sounds, and the cheerful clatter of breakfast plates being distributed on the deal board of the kitchen table.

In view of the feast to follow breakfast was to be a relatively small meal: porridge always bubbling away in the great pots, boiled eggs, golden-topped home-baked bread, and home-churned yellow butter; and since it was Christmas time, tea, still a luxury, but soon to become the Irish national beverage.

All this was on the table when Hugh came down, well washed, well combed, fresh and fit. As for Alice, there she was, as always; dewy-eyed, golden-haired, rosy-cheeked, clean and capable.

" Did you sleep well, Hugh ? "

" Never better, slept like a spinning top."

" Oh ! and I nearly forgot: a very happy Christmas ! " The way she emphasized the *very* Hugh knew that she was completely and utterly sincere; she knew something of his past—that he had rarely had the experience of anything resembling a happy Christmas.

Paddy arrived from the yard and the byres. Ducking the door lintel, as he came through, he simultaneously removed his hat. Apart from good manners, it was probably considered unlucky to cross the threshold while still wearing a hat. Good-mannered conventions frequently originate in superstition.

" Mornin', Hugh."

" Mornin', Paddy."

" An' a happy Christmas to you, Hugh. Seems no time since last Christmas; doesn't take long comin' round again. Ah' min' last Christmas well. One o' me best cows tuk it into her head to calve that day; an' was she slow ! Begod we thought we'd never get wer dinner. Then she took the milk-faver—God's truth, such a day ! But it'll not be like that this year, please God. Ah'll tell ye what we'll do you an' me: as soon as we get redd up here we'll take the guns an' the dogs an' we'll have a bit o' a hunt. Maybe we'll pick up a wood-cock, or a brace o' snipe, or somethin'—all good for the pot. Eh Alice ? Good mornin' for it—nice touch o' frost."

Hugh immediately offered to help with the " reddin' up."

" Not at all, man ! " Pat said. " Yer here on yer holidays, an' ye may as well enjoy yerself. Sure it'll take me no time. You just hang around here; an' keep Alice in crack for an hour or so."

Could Hugh have wished for anything better ?

Already the two were on a different footing: at that slightly shy stage when they had come to the realization that their initial momentary attraction was already blossoming into love. Alice understood that if Hugh were to make any advance toward her, physical or otherwise, she couldn't just treat him with the kind of banter she might have used toward some of the other fellows. For example, she couldn't say: " Och, away with ye, you don't know what love is; you're more in love with thon ould cow o' yours than ever ye'd be wi' me or any other girl." No, that wouldn't do; whatever Hugh said would be almost innocently sincere and serious.

Could he help her to wash up ? This was an unusual request; for in Ireland at that time a man's work was always outside: few would have offered to do anything about the house; that Hugh had made such an offer was in itself meant to be an intimate tribute to her: he wished to be close to her. She couldn't refuse the offer.

As she passed the cups, saucers, and plates to him to dry, each time she noticed how his fingers would linger against hers. And of course she would respond, not consciously but instinctively, for the touch of his fingers electrified her.

At last Hugh said:

" It was wonderful to waken up here this morning. It was wonderful to waken up knowing that I'd see you again. It was like a kind of dream. For a time I wondered was I really awake: was it just a dream ? "

For a moment Alice was a little taken aback. None of the local boys would have spoken to her like this. Love-making was a very formal routine affair and usually very practical.

A couple were deliberately thrown together; marriage was an arranged contract. There was little talk of dreams or even of love itself.

" Well, here I am Hugh; I'm no dream, just an ordinary country girl. I like you; I like you being here; and I hope we'll have some good times together before the holidays are over. Maybe we could take the horses out some day for a bit of a gallop up to the Knock Hill and back again. Would you like that ? "

Before Hugh had time to reply Paddy appeared at the door.

" Now Hugh," he said, " Ah'll show ye how to use a gun." He removed the fowling piece from its usual resting place above the mantel; and he also took down a couple of pouches, one containing the shot, and the other, gunpowder. He showed Hugh how to put in the powder, the shot, and the separating wads, the lot being rammed into place by the ramrod. He warned him never to put the cap into position until the gun was about to be brought into use.

Then off they went over hill and dale, bog and bush-land, with the frosted ground sparkling in the low sunlight, and crackling with every step. Though Hugh regretted leaving Alice, he enjoyed every moment in the crisp keen air. They rose a snipe or two on the bog, but they were not quick enough for these fast-moving birds. Near Loughorne Paddy brought down a duck; Hugh missed a hare; but later he hit an easier target—a rabbit. The kick of the too-closely held gun nearly knocked him off his feet, and gave him a sore shoulder for a week afterwards.

When at length they returned home with tired feet, glowing cheeks, and air-sharpened appetites, they found that the women folk had been busy. Soon the table was groaning with poultry and pickles, sprouts and spuds, home-cured ham, beef and beer, and all the essentials for a good Christmas meal without the additional trimmings that people expect in our day. In the soft light of coloured candles the whole presented an appearance attractive to the eye and appealing to the appetite.

One by one, and two by two, the Marys and Maureens, Bridgets and Bronaghs, Barneys and Benedicts, Johnnys and Joes, came in from town and townland; from around Loughbrickland and Loughorne, Ballynaskeagh, Ballyroney, and even Banbridge. With a few drinks inside, their preliminary awkwardness was soon replaced by relaxation and bonhomie. Initial conversation about crops and prices, weather and farming prospects generally turned to lighter matters: foolery and flirtations, gossip, and guesswork about neighbours' intentions.

Sitting opposite to Alice, Hugh would occasionally catch a sympathetic glance from her shining eyes, to be followed by an immediate lowering of those brown-fringed lids as she turned toward the man sitting beside her. He was a middle-aged widower farmer called Burns; he was paying more attention to Alice than Hugh would have wished; for the first time his whole being became shot through with the terrible pain of youthful jealousy.

After dinner there were games, stories, ballad singing, dancing, and fiddling. Hugh's humour was soon to be restored; when he met Alice in a lingering kiss beneath the mistletoe he knew what he must do; as far as he was concerned that kiss braced his resolve. Always a man of action, and always impetuous, he would waste no time. Action alone is one thing, impetuosity another, but when both are combined in the same individual the result may be fortunate or disastrous. Which was it to be in this case ?

The following day, Boxing Day, was to be a day off for Alice. Whatever meals there were would require little cooking. As promised she and Hugh would go for a canter on the horses. And so, when the usual house and farm chores had been completed, the two went out to the yard where Paddy already had the horses saddled and bridled.

" Take it aisy," he said, as he helped them to mount from the mounting stone, " we don't want to have to deal with any broken bones ! "

For Hugh this was heaven: a lovely companion with whom he was now completely in love; a good horse—he was no mean horseman—and unending miles of frost-bound fields for as far as one could see away to the blue Mourne domes piled against the lighter blue of a winter day.

Tired and flushed with the hard exercise they eventually drew rein beside a little spinney on high ground. While they were admiring the long view from Drumballyroney, with Rathfriland-on-the-Hill on one side, and to the right of it the Valley of the Clanrye meandering toward Newry, for the second time Hugh kissed his unreluctant Alice. What could she say ? What would any young unsophisticated girl say in such circumstances ?

" Oh, Hugh ! You—you. . . ." She was going to say " You shouldn't "; but instead she was almost surprised when she heard herself saying:

" I seem to have been waiting for this moment ever since we met." Perhaps an observer with a highly attuned ear might have detected in her voice a mixture of joy, fear, and and presentiment. There were so many things—so many difficulties. . . . Ah, well, all these problems could wait. In the meantime this was fun. Let's enjoy ourselves now. And so she returned his kiss with ardour.

Over the twelve days of Christmas there were many comings and goings. Visiting friends and relatives was the chief preoccupation; at every house you had to have cake and ale, or cake and wine; it was considered unlucky to leave any house without bite or sup. Fortunately Hugh's digestion was as strong as his frame; as he drank little, however, neither his temper nor his nerves suffered to quite the same extent as was the case with some of the other men, especially those who inhabited the local shebeens of an evening. Hugh manfully resisted all attempts to join in the evening libations; he would have enjoyed the fellowship, but not the whiskey, which he had not yet learned to enjoy. Besides, he needed no stimulants when there was the ever-present stimulation of Alice's warm presence at home.

Thus Alice and Hugh were often left to keep each other company in the evenings. It is difficult to know how anybody with any worldly wisdom could have been so blind as not to foresee the inevitable result. One night, as the two of them sat on the long settee at the fireside, Hugh said in his usual direct way:

" Alice, I love you. Will you marry me ? "

" Marry you, Hugh ! Marry you ! I don't know about marriage. I'm terribly fond of you; but what do I know about you ? We've only known each other for a few days." Then playing for time she said:

" You've just fallen in love with me because you haven't met any other girls. How do you know you love me anyhow? I saw Mary O'Hara givin' you a queer look at the barn dance the other night. You're a mighty handsome big fella; you could have any girl ye wanted. I heard them talkin' about you down in the village the other day. ' Thon fella,' one o' them said, ' Ah could take him to bed with me all right.' "

" An' there's another thing, Hugh; there's a terrible difference made here between Catholics and Protestants; if I said I was goin' to marry a Protestant there'd be hell let loose."

" Och, Alice, sure Ah know nothin' about religion. Ah'm neither Catholic nor Protestant; but Ah'm always willin' to learn. For you, Alice, Ah would do anything, anything in the wide world. As for knowin' nothin' about other girls: you're the first in me life, an' Ah believe it was a kind o' fate brought the two of us together—honest, Ah do ! Oh, Alice, ye must marry me—promise. Ah couldn't go on livin' without ye ! "

Then he began to tell her all about himself: about his early home of which he had been so fond, about the uprooting, and the devastating loneliness of his life in the wretched ruin beside the Boyne; of the terrible beatings and of his final fight and flight. He told it all with such power, insight, and dramatic effect that he brought the tears to her eyes; and almost before she quite realized what she was doing she had his head against her breasts. Her feelings at this point were so compounded of pity, passion and love that she could say none other than:

" Of course, of course, Hugh, I'll marry you. I can't see the way ahead now, but we'll get married no matter what happens."

CHAPTER 11

THE CROSSNESS

A ND a great deal was to happen. To say that the course
of true love never runs smoothly is not merely a cliché;
it is an epigram. Has there ever been an engagement without
some share of trouble and criticism ? The girl's parents may
not consider the man to be good enough for their wonderful
daughter, or the boy's parents may have similar thoughts
about the girl. The boy's prospects may be uncertain; the girl
may be considered a bit of a hussy and was out to get the
fellow; and " my dear she'll lead him a bit of a dance when
she gets him ! " A mother may even be jealous of her
daughter, and a father for his daughter, or a mother for her
son. Few engagements are completely free of all emotional
entanglements.

But when you have a pair, one of whom professes no
religion, while the other is a devout Catholic; and when the
boy has neither prospects, property, nor background, you have
all the conditions necessary for a domestic crisis. Bigotry was
rife in the eighteenth century, not only in Ireland but throughout Britain as a whole. Nowhere was it more rife than in
Northern Ireland which was not then a political entity, but
even so, it was a melting pot of various national and religious
ideas and ideals. And no matter how open-minded people
might profess to be, no matter how friendly they might be in
their day-to-day business and social contacts, marriage was
then—as it is now—a different matter when religious or racial
differences were involved.

When Hugh, with his usual directness, told Paddy that he
intended marrying his sister, Paddy was dumbfounded. Several

days of feasting, followed by heavy drinking at the shebeen, had created the worst possible temperamental conditions for the reception of such a devastating piece of news. Though up to this point the two young men had been the best of friends, suddenly there was a rupture. Paddy was called *Red* Paddy for more reasons than one:

" Marry me sister ! Who the hell do you think ye are to be talkin' about marryin' anybody let alone me sister ? Ye haven't a groat to call yer own; and what's more," he continued, " yer no Catholic; an' no sister o' mine's goin' to marry a Protestant bastard. Do ye hear ? " he said, coming menacingly closer, " yer not marryin' my sister ! Ye can put that in yer pipe an' smoke it."

" I love Alice; an' she loves me; an' what's more, we're for gettin' married no matter what you or anyone else may say. Ah may own no fields nor land, but Ah'm earnin' good money. Ah can support two o' us; an' as for not bein' a Catholic, Ah can soon learn about them, an' if Ah like them Ah'll join them; Ah'll do anything for Alice."

Though Red Paddy's temper was easily fanned into flame, it could cool again very rapidly. He was genuinely fond of Hugh, and sorry that this difference had arisen between them. Besides Hugh had refused to respond by losing his temper. In fact he had spoken with such calmness and resolution that he had surprised himself.

" Ah'm sorry, Hugh," said Paddy, " Ah didn't realize things had gone so far between yez. Ah'm a bit inclined to fly off the handle too aisy. There's nobody Ah'd like better to have as a brother-in-law, but there's goin' to be trouble— locally Ah mane. Ah'll tell ye what ye'll do: don't be too hasty about things. Ye'll be goin' back to Dundalk in a day or two. Think it over an' mebbe ye'll have changed yer mind when ye come back. In the meantime there's me han' on it; we'll still be good friends you an' me."

Hugh duly reported the conversation to Alice. With his usual boyish impetuosity he was all for an immediate marriage.

" To hell wi' the lot o' them Alice darlin', let's get married now. What's to prevent us ? "

But Alice, with the more mature outlook of a woman, counselled delay until they had all reached agreement. She also had the good sense to realize that Hugh might have been swept off his feet by their nearness, by their sympathy for each other, and by the whole spirit of Christmas. No, he needed time to reflect; and so did she for that matter; but away down in the depths of her mind she knew that, come what may, sooner or later the two of them would be bound together for as long as their lives would last.

" What's a week, Hugh, ye'll be that busy ye'll never notice the time passin'; an' it'll be the same for me an' at the week-end we'll be seein' each other again. Be a good lad, Hugh dear, think things over, don't do anything in a hurry; life lasts a long time ye know."

Uncertain of himself now, the inconsolable Hugh returned to his work for a week in which he scarcely knew what he was doing. After a day or two, however, the sun began to shine again; a day or two more and he would be back with her. He couldn't help thinking about the change that had come over him since his first journey to Ballynaskeagh; it was like the coming of spring after a long winter: a strange mixture of acute happiness coupled with a sort of deep delicious melancholy. Of course his master noticed the change:

" What ails ye Hugh ? Sometimes yer whistlin' an' singing like a spring bird; and at other times yer that sad ye'd think ye'd seen a ghost or sumpin'. Ah doubt ye must a found a wee lassie or sumpin'. Who is she ? Is she a good looker ? She'd need to be, for the likes o' a good-lookin' fella like yerself."

But Hugh took no notice, nor did he like the " coddin'." He was in two worlds now: the world of work and men on one hand, and a completely separate inner world on the other- a world in which only two people existed: Alice and himself.

At last Saturday came; when the foreman was giving him his wages he said:

" Things haven't been so good this week, Hugh; we didn't get as much lime away; and there were complaints from some of the best customers. There'll have to be an improvement next week."

" Ah'm sorry, John, Ah sure am. Ah wasn't feelin' quite meself; but things'll be better next week."

Back at the lodgings he made a quick change; and, without even waiting for his dinner he was off once more. As he drove up to the cross-roads, what did he see ? Ah, the flutter of a handkerchief ! Yes, there she was, Alice, looking as fresh and beautiful as ever. In a moment he had jumped from the gig; now there was no restraint between them; his arms were about her, and he was looking deep into her eyes with that utter and complete honesty which only lovers know.

But he saw that she was troubled. " Hugh, oh Hugh ! " she said, " there's something afoot; I don't quite know what it is; I think some of the local boys want to talk to you; for God's sake be careful ! "

" Come on, come on ! " Hugh cried. " Let's go away now, they can't stop us; we'll be half-way to Newry before they miss you. Come on, I say, before it's too late ! Some-body might see us here at any moment."

" No, no, Hugh, we can't do that; we'll have to do things in some better way. Where do you think we're going to go anyhow, and me with nothing to wear, or anything else ? Besides, I don't want to quarrel with Paddy; and I don't want you to quarrel with him: he's been a good brother to me; I'm very fond of him. Oh, Hugh, I'm afraid ! I'm afraid for you; I'm afraid for both of us. There's been a lot of talk since you were here last. Only the other day I was down in the village and I overheard one woman say to the other—she didn't see me:

" Did ye hear about the McClory hussy ? Believe she's got herself engaged to some fella or other. Don't know what he is: some kind o' a workin' man, or sumpin' from down south. Came up here on a lime cart. They say he's not even a Catholic. Suppose he thinks he's goin' to hang up his hat in the McClory place."

"Ye don't tell me," said the other woman, "ye never know what these young girls'll be up to nowadays. But she's a deep 'un thon McClory—too many boys—that's what I think."

"But it's not the women I'm afraid of, Hugh; they're only gossipin' an' talkin' an' they'd do that no matter who Ah was goin' to marry—it's the men, they're more dangerous."

Alice was right in this respect, as future events were to prove. The men were more dangerous, because some of them were being activated by deeper motives—motives that can often cause physical violence. Some of them were *after* Alice themselves, and they were raging that a stranger—almost a foreigner to them—had snapped her up under their very noses.

Hugh kept his thoughts to himself; he was not unused to physical violence; and he knew that if he were attacked he could give a pretty good account of himself. In any event there was nothing anybody could do to prevent him from carrying out his resolve to marry Alice. He knew that life without her would be intolerable. Many a young man has had similar thoughts; and it is all too easy to look back from the depths of age to think how foolish the young are; older people would say that time can change everything, and that there are many fish in the boundless ocean of time. But the current of life is not deflected by arm-chair reminiscence: it is immediate actions and reactions that count in the whole stream of human history.

In every crisis Hugh's own reactions were swift; once again his mind was made up; he'd face the lot of them; he'd present his case to them frankly and honestly; and if any of them wanted to fight the issue with him he'd put the issue to the test of fighting if necessary. As far as he was concerned, he had one case and one only: he loved Alice with all his heart and soul and body and strength. The religious issue was secondary; since he had no religion, and didn't care a shake of a lamb's tail whether James or William had won at the Boyne Battle, the matter had no relevance for him whatsoever; but as he was soon to find out, others had a more serious view about an event that was to cleave the men of Ulster for nigh on two centuries.

As they walked up the hill together hand in hand, Hugh said:

" Ah'm goin' to face the lot o' them before Ah go back."

" All right, Hugh, if your mind's made up there's nothing more to be said, but do be careful. Say what you have to say; and leave it at that; fightin' won't help. I know Paddy's fond of you and he's gentle and kind underneath, but he can't stand against the whole countryside. This is where we live and have to make a living; we can't fight with our own friends. They've all been at me since you went away, tryin' to persuade me that Ah'm doin' the wrong thing; that Ah should marry a decent Catholic; and that Ah'd live to regret it if Ah didn't. Even the priest called the other day; he's a nice man, the Father, ye'd like him Hugh. I told him that religion didn't matter; that the only thing that mattered was our love for each other. I'm afraid—I—I—cried; but in the end he agreed that maybe Ah was doin' the right thing in followin' the dictates of my heart."

When they reached home Paddy was there, and there were no hard feelings. Out went the hand of welcome as usual.

" Grand to see ye, Hugh. How have ye been since ? Ah haven't been along to the kiln for some time; all the limin's been done; an' we're not doin' any buildin' at the moment. How are things below ? "

" Rightly, Paddy, rightly," Hugh replied, adopting the local vernacular. " But to tell the truth Ah'm a bit worried about all this fuss about Alice and me gettin' married."

" Ah know, Ah know, but Hugh, it's not just as aisy as ye think. Ye see there's been a terrible friction here for years between Catholics and Protestants—not between friends an' neighbours," he hastened to add, " but more in a general sort o' way if ye understand. When a lot o' boys get together on the one side an' a lot on the other, there can be trouble."

Lovers always imagine that their affair is different from any other; so when Hugh said: " Listen, Paddy, they don't understand ! " he was echoing the heartfelt cry of all the misunderstood young people in love throughout all the ages. People simply did not understand that they were in love to a degree far above the ordinary.

" Tell you what Paddy, if you would get a few of the boys in, mebbe I could explain, an' mebbe we'd all understand each other better."

" Sumpin' in what ye say; might be a good idea. Tell ye what; Ah'll get a few o' them along to-morrow after Mass; an' ye can have a crack with them. When they see the sort o' man ye are; and when they know that you an' Alice are determined to get spliced mebbe they'll think different."

But the optimism of Red Paddy and Hugh found no justification. Not only had some of the men imbibed pretty freely before their arrival in the McClory kitchen, but in addition there were bottles and glasses on the table—an almost inevitable complement to every meeting; and one calculated to give the proceedings more spirit in both the metaphysical and substantive meaning of the term.

" Mornin', men," was Hugh's restrained and cordial greeting as he sat down in the chair reserved for him at the head of the table.

" Mornin' yerself," one of the men—self-appointed spokesman—replied without any show of cordiality.

" Pleased to meet you all," Hugh said, " Ah asked ye to meet me here just to tell ye that Alice and me are in love with each other; an' we hope to get married as soon as possible."

Before he could say anything further one of the men passed over the bottle with the usual request: " Have a drink."

" No, thank you," Hugh said, " Ah don't drink whiskey."

" Don't drink whiskey ! What sort o' a man are ye ? Mebbe ye think we're not good enough to drink with."

"So yer thinkin' o' marryin' Alice, are ye? Now just before we go any further: what religion do ye profess? Just tell us straight are ye Protestant or Catholic?"

By this time the men, fired with strong whiskey, were becoming more aggressive. Hugh, without any whiskey, was, to say the least of it, becoming slightly nettled at the turn things were taking. This interrogation was not to his liking, and was not what he expected.

None-the-less he still managed to retain his self-control, so he answered as politely as possible:

"Ah never had any opportunity to study religion; Ah know nothin' about it. Ah can honestly say Ah'm neither Catholic nor Protestant."

"Quit hedgin' man! Which are ye?"

Hugh preserved a stubborn silence. Then one of the men opposite leaned over and in a menacing way said:

"If yer on our side let's hear ye curse King William!"

By this time Hugh's gorge was beginning to rise. Alice saw the tell-tale signs. She knew there was danger ahead; she stiffened, and the next minute she screamed as she heard Hugh say in measured terms:

"Curse King William! How can I curse a man who's dead and one I never knew: I'd as soon curse the Pope!"

There was pandemonium: the dogs of war were loosed. The terms used two hundred years ago were the same as those employed up to the present day, and they have been the subject of countless graffiti ever since. Spurred into violent action by such terms, and with all normal restraint loosened by whiskey, the men were capable of anything.

Hugh felt as though he had been struck by a thunderbolt, but with shaken teeth and blood flowing from his nose and lips, he still had the strength of ten. While he heard somebody shouting: "Kill the bastard of a blackmouth!" he gave one mighty heave hurling his assailants this way and that, as he literally crashed through the drunken mass to the open door-way. He was followed by Alice; the two didn't stop running intil they reached the plantation of pines on a " forth " at some distance from home.

" Oh, Hugh, Hugh, Hugh, didn't I warn ye ! " Alice said breathlessly, nearly sobbing with fear for her lover, and horror from what she had seen.

No one followed; they could see that easily from their observation point among the pine needles. Probably the men—decent men at heart—were now thoroughly ashamed of what they had done. No doubt, too, Paddy had by this time mollified them.

Hugh remained silent while Alice, using her handkerchief and water from a nearby stream, cleaned his wounds, and restored normality to his throbbing temples. Then his arms were about her, and the two of them swore eternal fidelity, and everlasting love, come what may.

" My dear, my dear, my dear ! you'll have to go now but you'll be back again soon, I know you will. You'll have to come back, for I'll need you now more than ever. Don't stay away long, Hugh ! "

" O' course me darlin' lovely Alice, Ah'll be back, don't you worry; an' don't let any o' them fellas worry ye either. They'll be tryin' harder than ever now to put ye off the notion o' marryin' me; but we'll be married all right, don't you fret. There's only one thing, though: after what happened to-day Ah don't think Ah could ever become a Catholic."

" Forget about all that, Hugh; put it right out of your mind. When we are married I'll do as you say: your ways will be my ways." The same affirmation had been made three thousand years before by one whose faith had been different from that of the man she was about to marry; it had probably been made a million times since in similar circum-stances; to Hugh at that moment it was a balm in Gilead to his tortured mind.

For a little longer they held each other; and then as the evening sun, now fast sinking behind the Armagh hills, began to gild all the fields and valleys, the woods and waterways of that quiet land, Hugh once more headed south.

All through the night he walked, but what did it matter? Sleep would have been denied him anyhow. As Hugh wound his lonely way along leafy lanes, no longer leafy except underfoot where the slow after-summer decay was still at work creating a squelchy mulch, he would presently see the lights of the castled, hill-top town of Rathfriland. From Rathfriland he would follow the valley of Clanrye to Newry. Once out of Newry he would have the Narrow Water as his guide; and from there the sea-girt edge of Carlingford would map his course to Mount Pleasant.

His heart and head were so occupied that the miles dropped behind him as easily as if he were a bird on the wing. Normally tiredness was a sensation to which he was almost unaccustomed; in this cool January air, in spite of his recent physical and emotional stress, he scarcely realized he had a body. He never stayed to rest, save once at an inn outside Newry where a glass of milk and a hunk of bread gave him the necessary sustenance for the final effort. The dawn was already beginning to ring the eastern sky beyond Man and Mourne when at last he saw the glowing smoke from Mount Pleasant; and there for the second and last time in his life he laid him down in its warm and friendly ambience.

Soon—all too soon—the carts began to rumble up the rough lime-whitened path, to be followed by the clang and clatter of picks, hammers and shovels, as the hard calcined lime was broken, shovelled, and loaded, while more and more of the fuel-mixed unburned stone was put into the kilns.

Hugh worked; but had no heart for his work. He thought to himself " what a fool Ah was; why didn't Ah control me temper; an' all would have been well? Why, oh why, did Ah allow meself to be provoked? Sure if Ah'd just kept quiet no harm would have been done; things would have settled down; an' they'd have begun to accept the fact that the two of us were goin' to marry. Now the fat's in the fire: we'll be the talk of the country! Sooner or later them fellas 'll want to get their own back on me; or, worse still, mebbe they'll try to take it out on Alice. Oh, what the hell have Ah done? "

While he was immersed in these gloomy thoughts, in a kind of daze he heard a voice shouting:

" Hie, there, Brontë ! what do ye think yer up to ? There's half a dozen carts there waitin' to be filled ! "

" Right, John, hie there boys get them carts loaded up ! " While the loading was taking place one of the customers lifted a lump of lime, examined it, and then said curtly: " Thon lime's not half burned. Ah'm not goin' back wi' that, or Ah'd get me head in me hands."

This was only the beginning of a whole series of complaints. Men were to take loads home only to find that the lime would not slake down properly; it was useless for certain purposes; for example, for building: you couldn't make mortar from unburnt lime. Also many of the carts came from the North, especially from around the Newry area. News spreads quickly among country folk; thus it was that exaggerated reports of Hugh's behaviour on the day of the ill-fated meeting in the McClory kitchen began to spread among Hugh's Catholic workmates. He was accused of being a Protestant bigot who had cursed the Pope.

And men were heard to say: " Don't know what's gone wrong with Brontë—not like what he used to be. Damn the bit o' crack ye can get out o' him now. Min' the time he was the great one for telling stories. An' what do ye think ? He's teaching himself to read—to *read* Ah tell ye boys. He spends his nights there in the light o' the kiln fingerin' away at some oul holy book or other. Thon wumman o' his must 'a turned his head completely ! What does a lime man want wi' learnin' to read ? "

But Hugh was happy—morosely perhaps, but in his own way he was happy. At week-ends, on Sundays, he and Alice continued to meet in secret; but oh how sweet a secret meeting can be ! And when the pair feel they are two against the world the attraction between them grows in proportion to the resistance against them. And so when the lovers met in the

glades, glens, and hazel groves around Emdale and Ballynaskeagh, each meeting was an unforgettable memory. One of
their meeting places is still known locally as " The Lovers'
Arbour."

CHAPTER 12

LOUGHORNE LOVERS

THEN they were betrayed by a serving man who carried notes between them. Once again feelings boiled up. Down in Loughbrickland the gossipmongers were hard at it.

" Did ye hear about thon Alice McClory ? "

" No Ah didn't, Ah thought they'd quit ! "

" So did I; but Ah hear they're coortin' away as hard as ever."

" Ye don't tell me ! "

" Aye, Ah do; and what do ye think the cheeky hussy's doin' ? " Here the lady concerned drew closer to her confederate and said in a loud whisper:

" She's been meetin' him down in the Glen within a stone's throw of her own house; an' Ah believe the kissin' an' huggin' was disgraceful. Sumpin' 'll have to be done about it. It shouldn't be allowed in a dacent community like this."

" Who towl ye all this ? "

" Who towl me ? Sure it's common knowledge. Ye know that fella that works for them there; he was in the habit o' passin' notes berween them when he took the cart down to the lime works. *He* gave the show away ! "

" Lawkes a mussey ! the cheek o' them. The girl has lost her head altogether. An' ye know there's a decent Catholic widower—Burns—a good solid man with lands an' cattle; he'd marry her to-morrow if he got the chance."

" A very suitable match; we'll all have to get round her to see if we can't knock a bit o' sense into her. What about that brother o' hers, what's he doin' about it ? "

" Ah don't know nothin' about that; he's far too much of a softie anyhow; an' Ah believe he's thick with the fella Hugh — whatever ye call him. If I was him Ah'd give the girl what for; an' tell her she'll have to marry Burns or get out."

" Well Ah don't know, what's everybody's business is nobody's business; but Ah hope somebody makes her see sense. Good-bye Missus. Ah have to be home to make the oul man his dinner ! "

" Good-bye to yourself, an' may God go with ye ! "

So ended this typical conversation, but Hugh's troubles were far from ending: efforts were certainly being made to dislodge him from his job; while at the same time almost intolerable pressures were being brought to bear on Alice to force her to marry Farmer Burns. But she was a girl of spirit and other ideas were beginning to form in her mind.

While Alice was having to withstand pressures, Hugh was the unwilling recipient of jeers and insults.

" Have a good time last night; yer lukin' tired enough anyhow," a man would call at him with a bawdy leer.

Or another would say: " How's the readin' goin' ? Suppose ye'll soon be at the preachin' an' teachin'; ye'll be tryin' to convert the lot of us before long."

But Hugh refused to be drawn; if eventually he had to fight again, he would do so; he would choose his own time—not now for he didn't wish to precipitate his departure which he knew was bound to come before long.

And come it did; sooner than he expected. One week-end when he was away, a man who had promised to fire the kilns for him deliberately allowed them to go out; when the carts pulled in on Monday morning the lime, which should have been ready, was still in the form of hard lumps of limestone.

The boss sent for Hugh; he said: " You're fired." That was all, no word of thanks, no handshake, golden or other-wise—just this simple imperative against which Hugh had no redress. And so once again we find him on the road, this time *en route* for Newry where eventually he was to present himself at the hiring fair. He was hired to—or hired himself

to—whichever is the more correct way of putting it—a Mr. James
Harshaw of Donoughmore at the princely sum of £6 per
annum plus board and lodging. What could a poor, out-of-
work fellow do but accept? As it turned out his acceptance was
a turning point in his fortunes.

Now if you were to go into the beautifully situated village
of Rostrevor at the southernmost extremity of the Mourne
Mountains where they look across toward Carlingford and
Hugh's late place of employment, you would find within the
village enclosure an ancient graveyard known as the Crag
Graveyard. Searching among the old monuments and head-
stones there, you would discover one bearing the inscription:

" Robert Martin, son of Samuel Martin and Jane Harshaw,
born at Lough-horne. . . ."

The Jane Harshaw referred to was none other than the
accomplished and intelligent daughter of the Mr. James
Harshaw who hired Hugh Brontë at the hiring fair in Newry.
Not only did she have a considerable influence on Hugh, but
he appears to have had some influence on her. He probably
told her all about his boyhood experiences; this in turn led
her to realize that all was not for the best in the best of all
possible worlds; indeed she was to discover that because of the
machinations of selfish men, many people without rights or
privileges were to be denied even a modicum of what life had
to offer. Her thinking appears to have been passed on to her
second son, brother of Robert Martin referred to above;
he—" Honest John Martin "—took action, becoming the
associate and friend of John Mitchell. The two were prominent in The Rising of the Young Irishmen; in consequence they
were exiled, but later pardoned. Honest John, and his brother
Robert, lived at Kilbroney House, a short distance from where
this book is being written. John could have been a man of
substance but preferred to live for his people, as his mother
had done before him.

No sooner did Alice come to know of the whereabouts of
Hugh than she would often, of an evening, put spurs to her
horse and gallop him over to Loughorne. There she would

find her lover by the lakeside, busying himself with various jobs until he would hear the welcome sound of galloping hooves.

Did the Harshaws know what was going on ? It is difficult to be sure: one can only guess that they must have had some inkling. How could Hugh and Alice have walked the shingled shore at Warrenpoint, or the sandy shores at Newcastle, without the Harshaws being in the know to some extent ? But they were humane and human; they understood.

They understood Hugh to a surprising extent; they mothered him, and helped him to improve his reading. His handsome appearance was in his favour; but their interest was not merely physical; they were quick to recognize an intelligence unusual in a man of his standing. With them Hugh was to find a spirit of service based on friendship. Can true service be based on any other spirit ?

For thousands of years since the days of the wolf-excluding forts, or forths, the Irish farm has been an enclosed unit inside which families, servants, and even animals have laid themselves down under the same roof. Through all the millenniums, centuries and decades the custom has tended to persist: the farmer, his family of two, even three, generations, and his servants, have fed together, and slept, if not in the same room, at least under the same roof.

The Harshaws were, measured by the standards of the time, large and good farmers. Hugh usually fed with them, farmed with them, drove with them, and even worshipped with them in the ancient Donoughmore Church. It was probably here that he first became acquainted with religion as practised in the Established Church—the form that he and his family were to accept and adhere to in later years.

Hugh still continued to meet Alice occasionally; more often, however, they were compelled to communicate only by the passage of notes of love left in the hollow of an old tree near the lake; unfortunately the tree—" Brontë's Post-box "— and the lake, Loughorne, have long since disappeared. It was

I

literally a red-letter day for Hugh when he found a note from his beloved inside the ancient bough. Quickly he would tuck it inside his tunic; and, when an opportunity offered he would read it at leisure, lying on his back in the hay loft. The notes, scented only with the scent of old wood, gave him almost as much joy as contact with Alice's rose-red lips.

But one day he received a shock; a letter read:

Dearest,

Something happened a day or two ago; I thought I ought to tell you about it in case you heard from somebody else. They have been getting at me to such an extent lately that I had no option other than to agree to marriage with Mr. Burns.

(At this point Hugh's heart gave such a bound that he could scarce continue reading.)

But, darling, I want you to know that no word of love has passed between me and Mr. Burns, nor have I allowed him even to touch me. You must believe me about this.

But oh, Hugh, my dear, my dearest ! I must see you soon ! If you can possibly manage, be at the Lake's side to-morrow about dusk. I have a plan. In case anything happens to prevent our meeting, try again the next day, and the next.

With all my love,
Alice.

Hugh spent a sleepless night; he could scarcely contain himself until dusk the next day. In spite of Alice's protestations and reassurance he was worried. A promise to marry was something not to be taken lightly, especially in Ireland, where an unwritten bond between families was sacrosanct. No matter what Alice had in mind, circumstances could place matters outside her control.

It was therefore with a beating heart that Hugh found himself digging at drains in the low field running down to

Loughorne. As the evening hush stole over the land, and the tree shadows began to lengthen on the lake, his ear became attuned to its finest pitch of hearing. Ah, there it was, the sound of a horse trotting in the distance ! Soon she was there looking fairer than ever in the half-light of evening. What a beautiful sight, Hugh thought, as he saw her in the lake's reflected light, swing easily down, while she allowed her mount to take long deep gulps of the clear, clean water. While she was tying her horse to the post-box tree, Hugh moved quickly around to her side. As they kissed and embraced he knew that all his fears were groundless; she was his; she never could, nor would, belong to another.

Then in a whisper, and with almost uncontrolled excitement, she told him her plan.

" Listen, Hugh, this is what I want you to do. . . ."

CHAPTER 13

THE ELOPEMENT

IN the meantime at the Ballynaskeagh McClory home, things were moving forward with increasing impetus toward the big event. Red Paddy was determined to show them. He had listened long enough to all the tongue-wagging. Yes, he would show them ! His sister would have a wedding fit for a queen. He had money tucked away, saved for this objective and this alone; money ! nobody need talk to him about expense ! He'd blue the lot. By God ! he'd give her a wedding that would be talked about all over the country for years to come.

He had been to the lime kilns where he had purchased a load of first-class, well-burnt lime—not like the stuff that fellow Brontë had been giving him not so long ago. No, this was the best: clean, easily slaked. From Newcastle he had drawn a load of lovely white sea sand; none o' yer muddy brown stuff from a pit.

" Never mind the spuds, boys, they'll not rot; we're whitewashin' to-day. Go on Seumas, you up the ladder there ! Me an' Barney down below ! Right boys—make her as white as the angels in heaven ! "

What a whitewashing there was ! When they had finished, and the limewash had dried, the whole house gleamed like driven snow. As for the brass knocker, and the door handle. Paddy polished these until, as he put it himself, he could see his distorted face, like one o' them ould demons from hell. When they had sanded, smoothed and rolled the path, " it looked that clean that ye could a' ate yer spuds off it."

Inside the house Alice and her helpers brushed, and cleaned, polished and burnished until you would have needed a microscope to detect a spot of dust, and until pots and pans, ornaments and bric-à-brac scintillated and shone like meadow dewdrops touched by the sun on a summer morning.

Soon there was to be a succession of carters with cart-loads of crates and containers. There were barrels of beer from Banbridge, whiskey and wine from Dundalk and Dublin, flour from the flour mills, currants and raisins from local retailers, tea, tobacco, and snuff, nuts, apples—aye ! and even grapes and oranges. Where they all came from nobody knew, but everything possible was done to delight the eye and stimulate the appetite of even the most discerning gourmet. Few in that part of the country had ever seen the like before.

Oh, happy, happy day ! Was it to be or not to be ? Alice didn't quite know; but of one thing she was certain, it would be vastly different from anything anybody could have anticipated. Nevertheless preparations were to go ahead exactly as everybody would have anticipated. Day by day the dressmaker would arrive with needles and thread, pins, scissors, measuring tape and all the other dressmaker's accessories. Each evening there would be the trying on of this, that, and the other piece of bride's and bridesmaid's apparel, until it came to the final evening when Alice appeared on the balcony above the kitchen clad in her bridal gown. The *Ah's* and *Oh's* from the women present were a sufficient tribute to the bride's rare beauty and the effectiveness of her adornment.

It was Alice's last evening before her free, single life was to be exchanged for one of service to her husband, his farm, and the many children that would probably be consequent on her marriage. Thus she was relieved of all kitchen duties. History does not record what she did; but one could hazard a guess that she prayed and prayed as few about-to-be brides ever prayed before.

Down in the kitchen broth bubbled, puddings steamed, two great turkeys, ham, and beef spluttered in their buttered pans and pots in as lively a fashion as any such goodies had ever previously roasted, broiled and boiled in cottage or castle kitchen.

By the midnight hour all was ready. The bride—God bless her ! as many said—had finished her gown, and was supposedly asleep with her happy dreams; and the groom, relaxing somewhat from his normal gravity, was having a bit of a stag party with his closest friends, who were doing their best to ensure that he would hardly know what he was up to when the morrow dawned.

And when the morrow dawned fine and clear everyone, save the bride, were up betimes. The first big event of the day was the ride for the Bridal Broth—a race from Knock Hill to the yard. Riders, with their horses freshly groomed, and with harness fairly gleaming, were assembled at the wild, rocky fort of the cairn-topped hill. At the word " Go ! " they were off: a jostling, dust-enshrouded mass of horses and riders and, after the first mile or so, riderless horses galloping madly down the rough white road with cracking crops, dug-in heels, and shouts of enouragement to their respective mounts. From every hill-top round about there were shouts of " Come on Paddy ! Come on Barney ! Come on Mike ! " or from the more facetious: " If ye don't put yer heels in him Mac, it's you'll be carryin' *him* home ! " Eventually the leaders, with Burns at the head, mounted on a great black steed, clattered bravely into the yard where they were presented with liberal libations of McClory whiskey.

Then they stood by their bit-champing horses waiting for the bridal gig to depart.

They waited and waited; their horses and themselves becoming more and more restive. Like a cloud blotting out the sun a rumour began to go around. Where was the bride ? She was nowhere to be found. Good heavens ! Surely ? Surely ? No, she couldn't have done. . . . Anybody seen the bride ? " Yes," someone said, " she had dressed; then donning a cloak, she had decided to go for a ride to clear her head after a sleepless night."

She must have had an accident !

First off the mark was Burns on his black charger. He was followed by another, and another, and finally by every man who could find a mount. But they might as well have saved their horses and themselves: though they scoured every acre of the lands and townlands around Emdale, Ballynaskeagh, and out toward Knockiveagh, Ballynafern and Banbridge, neither sight nor sound of Alice could be found.

At last a messenger arrived with supplies from Banbridge. Yes, he had seen Alice riding behind a gentleman; they were galloping hell for leather along the Bann side. Where exactly had he seen them ? In what direction were they heading ? The poor fellow was almost bemused with questions, and nearly crushed with the press of men, women, and horses around him.

Another rider came galloping down the road; this time a boy astride Alice's mare. And he had a message, to wit, a note from Alice: it read in effect:

Dear Friends,

I just want to ask your forgiveness for all that has happened; but it had to happen. How could I enter into a marriage with Mr. Burns when I loved another man so deeply that I could never have been happy without him.

Hugh Brontë and I have just been married at Magherally Church, and I am now Mrs. Brontë. I apologize to Mr. Burns; he is a good man; I am sure he will understand.

I ask you to go on with the wedding party; and please enjoy yourselves as though everything had taken place as arranged. I ask for your blessing, and hope you will drink to the health of Mr. and Mrs. Hugh Brontë.

With love to you all.
Alice.

At last it was out: the plan had been unfolded. The whole affair had been perfectly organized. Alice was to feign a headache or something of the sort, to give her an excuse for her unusual early morning pre-wedding ride. Hugh would be waiting for her a few miles away. Alice's horse would be handed over to the care of a young fellow; and a previously apprised sympathetic parson would be waiting to marry them at the old Magherally Church some five miles away on the north side of the Bann River.

Alice and Hugh were often to describe that ride in later years. Everything worked out in their favour; there were no hitches. As soon as Alice arrived at the trysting place she quickly dismounted from her own horse, and with the agility of a born rider, she sprang into the pillion seat behind Hugh; then away, away across grass field and fallow, hedge and hollow, ditch and drain, until they espied the meandering silver waters of the Bann River. Having followed its course for three miles or so they crossed the ford at Bally Ievey, then up the hill and to the right to Magherally Church where a kindly parson quickly performed the marriage ceremony.

Though they were sufficiently realistic to be aware that there were still breakers ahead on the matrimonial seas, they had steered their barque well, and had conquered. How well they deserved their final bliss can only be appreciated by those who have had to fight every inch of the way to ultimate happiness.

How were all these arrangements made? We can only speculate. As we saw earlier Alice told Hugh all about what she had in mind; and there is every likelihood that Hugh must have had something to do with the organization. It doesn't seem very feasible that Alice, as a Catholic, could have been in a position to communicate with the reverend gentleman at Magherally. He, on the other hand, would have been only too pleased to accept the pair into the Protestant fold. Maybe the Harshaws, being members of the Donoughmore Church, might have been able to arrange something through their own rector. Certain it is, however, that such a complicated plan could not have been carried into effect without the willing co-operation of sympathizers.

Back at the McClory home there was pandemonium. Apart from the saner and more gentle-minded people—and the more temperate—there were those who would have had the two arrested, convicted, and subjected to almost any indignity provided they were made to understand the enormity of their sin. Among those who remained silent were the most affected: Mr. Burns, Red Paddy, and the priest.

When at last it was found possible to herd them all to the table—for, come what may, the inner man had to be satisfied—there was so much babbling, talking, commiserating, and complaining that the Tower of Babel would have seemed silent in comparison. But with an excellent dinner in front of them, before long even the most vociferous began to become quieter; and, not a few thought with admiration about the courage and skill with which Alice had won her way to marriage with the man she loved. In doing so she had also won the hearts of many present.

Then the priest stood up—the white-haired old priest who had seen more of the world and its ways than most. He said:

" My friends, you came here to celebrate a wedding, and a wedding we have celebrated truly and well, thanks to the generosity of the McClory family. But, I might add, it's not the wedding we expected to take place.

" My friend, Mr. Burns—a decent man if ever there was one—has been disappointed; and I feel sure we all have the greatest sympathy for him. No doubt my friend loved Alice in his own way; but didn't we all love Alice in much the same way ? For Alice is a beautiful girl, and a capable girl; and is there a man among us here who could put his hand on his heart and say honestly that he didn't love Alice ? Not one of you could—myself included.

" To love a girl in a more or less dispassionate and admiring way is one thing; but to love her with the whole ardour of youth is another; and there is no doubt about it that Alice and

Hugh Brontë are so deeply in love that they could never have been happy without each other.

" Please don't take it amiss, Mr. Burns, if I say to you that you are well out of it. Alice never wished to marry you, but she came under great pressure; to keep the peace she gave you her promise at a time when she thought she had lost her Hugh for ever. No sooner did she find out that Mr. Brontë was back in the district than she was filled with regrets and remorse; not everybody knew this, but I did.

" To be married to a young girl who loves another is not an enviable state; and remember she will still be young when you are old; she will still need life when you will require a nurse. We all agree that you are a fine, upstanding, and handsome man for your age; but at your age the years move on with ever increasing rapidity. Some day you might find yourself too old for both your wife and a young family.

" Let me say this, however: you are not too old for a wife—one a wee bit nearer your own age. And here I'm going to let you into a secret: you'd be a right match for one or two comfortable wee women around here: you with your handsome appearance, your tidy wee bit o' land, your several head of sleek cattle, and your healthy flocks of sheep and birds. It may be an old saw, but it's none the less true, that there are as good fish in the sea as ever came out of it; and when the good fish is, metaphorically speaking, a woman with a nice bit o' land that marches on yours, what more could you want ?

" And now, my friends, we are gathered here to-day to celebrate the marriage of two of our young people who were meant for each other, and whom God has brought together. They have accepted a different faith, but who are we to judge the thoughts and the working of the mind of the Almighty ? Don't forget that there are good Catholics, and bad Catholics; there are good Protestants and bad Protestants. We are not concerned with labels; we are concerned with men and women, and the whole spread of Christianity. God will judge us not by our labels, but by our lives.

" And now, in the true spirit of the Master whom we serve, let us welcome this splendid and courageous young pair into our community, always remembering that maybe it is the divine purpose that something great may result from their union. The success of a marriage depends, not merely on the young people concerned, but on those around and about them: on their relatives, friends and neighbours.

" The other day, when out walking in our beloved hills, I happened to notice an unusually beautiful sunset. Not only did it blaze with saffron, green, gold and red, but the whole sky in every quarter was ringed with bright colour. I couldn't help thinking that in this there was a message: that all the beauty and graciousness of life is not merely at the focus; we are ringed around it. So in our small community here let us accept everybody, irrespective of class or creed, within the full circle of God's love and charity.

" Ladies and gentleman, I ask you to rise and drink a toast:

" Mr. and Mrs. Hugh Brontë; may they have God's blessing and every happiness here in Ballynaskeagh."

" Mr. and Mrs. Hugh Brontë—God bless them ! "

When they sat down there was scarcely a dry eye amongst all the relatives and friends.

While all this was happening in the year of Our Lord 1776 Mr. and Mrs. Hugh Brontë were gaily speeding—if speeding is the right word in those leisurely days—in a hired gig on their way to Warrenpoint where they were to spend their honeymoon.

CHAPTER 14

WARRENPOINT HONEYMOON

IN the year 1776 there must have been very little of Warrenpoint as we know it to-day: probably some thatched
cottages, the Windmill, the Crown Hotel maybe, and the old
Oyster Saloon; and a few Georgian better-class houses may
have already made their appearance along the sea-front facing
the sea-margined slopes of the Cooley Mountains.

" Look at that ! " said Alice as they trotted along the
shallow pass of the Mournes, and saw for the first time the
gold-suffused Lough framed in the mountainy gap toward
Rostrevor. " Isn't it beautiful ? "

And of course it was beautiful, as Hugh was quick to agree.
Apart altogether from the static billows of the Mourne
Mountains, the wooded slopes, and this superb view of the
sea-lough of Carlingford, how could any young man, sitting
in a gig with his dream girl, have seen anything that was not
beautiful ? At that moment Hugh would have seen beauty in
back-street Belfast.

The highest point passed, the horse was pulled in a little
for the long downhill walk along the tree-covered road to
the village of Rostrevor with the domed height of Slieve Bán
rising, as it seemed, almost sheer up from the narrow-streeted
village at the sea's edge. Soon they were once more trotting
along the storm-rutted road toward Warrenpoint. It was one
of those rare evenings when the sea was so calm that its mirror-
like surface reflected the land masses almost as though the
mythical city of Cahir Linn still existed in the Lough's bottom.

It was not difficult for the passing traveller to find lodgings
in those days when such food as the sea and land could provide

was usually available; and when people were prepared to put up with conditions and discomforts which would now be unacceptable. But they were fortunate and comfortable enough in the privacy of their tiny sea-fronted room.

As they prepared for bed on their first night together they had neither inhibitions nor embarrassments. Alice removed her pins, undid her buttons, and took down her hair as though she were a bride of yesteryear. They felt as natural in each other's naked presence as only those deeply in love can be. They needed neither sex education nor family planning. In each other's arms they were conscious only of each other. If and when children came they would come as a gift, for every child would be a helper in youth and a solace in old age: such was the attitude of their time and circumstance.

The following morning Hugh was up betimes. He washed in cold water from the jug, and stole softly from the room so as not to disturb Alice who was sleeping like a child. Down at the harbour he looked appraisingly at a four-master loading cattle for Liverpool; he was interested because it was something he had taken part in at Drogheda. How easy it was now to look back on that wretched past from which he had been separated for ever. How happy he was now ! Oh, God, how happy he was ! As he looked across the Narrow Water; as the eyes of his mind penetrated the mountains, and all the country beyond, he saw himself back once more, the little boy beside the Boyne; strangely the pain of his experiences was disappearing, so that he could now think almost nostalgically about those far-off unhappy days. The truth is that looking down from the heights of his present happiness, all he could see were the fair plains, the meadows, and the wooded hills surrounding the meandering Boyne from Slane to Laracor. " I must take Alice there some day ": that was the thought in his mind.

The thought of Alice made him throw his arms in the air and shout: " Yipee ! " Then he took a great gulp of the fresh sea-air pouring up from Carlingford to Clanrye; and he ran home to Alice's arms, and breakfast.

If you were to ask Hugh later what the two of them did during the remaining honeymoon days, could he have told you? All he remembered was a jumble of joy. Of course they would have walked up the Bridal Path to see the famous Coronation Stone on which the heads of the Mac Guiness clan were crowned; of course they would have looked with awe at Lassara's Leap, the gloomy Norman tower house, Narrow Water Castle, from which Lassara leaped to the ghostly arms of her harp-playing lover. Inevitably they would have made the trip to Rostrevor and then up to the Cloghmore Stone; and they would have initialled the stone in accordance with the centuries-old custom of those in love. Looking at the monster stone Hugh might have said: " Sowl an' he was a boy ! " referring, of course, to the legend which both of them, in the absence of any geological knowledge, would doubtless have believed.

Standing up there hand in hand, Hugh would have been able to point in the direction of the scene of his more recent labours at the Mount Pleasant kiln behind castellated Carling-ford. Though he had been happy enough there, he would have felt slightly nettled about his summary expulsion, especially when he knew the fault lay, to a large extent, with himself. Still, if he had never been there he'd never have met his brother-in-law, Red Paddy; and he would not now have been holding the hand of the loveliest girl in the world.

" All that's past; what of the future, Hugh ? " Alice said, interrupting her man's flow of thought; and, like many another woman, getting down to the practicalities of life.

This was something Hugh had pushed into the background. In the meantime he wished to enjoy their idyll to the full, though he knew the problem would have to be faced sooner or later.

" Och, to hell with the future ! Let's enjoy ourselves now," was Hugh's rejoinder, as for the first time he became slightly irritated. After a moment's reflection he quickly recovered his poise, realizing that Alice's question was reasonable.

"We've only a day or so left, Hugh dear, and it's something we'll have to face."

"Don't Ah know, me pet; but there's no need to worry. First Ah have to finish me term with the Harshaws—you *know* that; an' Ah don't think they'll ever see me stuck. You'll have to go back to Paddy for a wee while; an Ah'll have to go on livin' with the Harshaws, but we'll be seein' other every day."

"Aye, Hugh, but we couldn't go on livin' like that for ever; sooner or later we'll have to find a wee place of our own."

"Don't Ah know, an haven't Ah made up me mind long ago that never again will Ah work for a boss. Ah'm goin' to be me own master. We're both hard workers, you an' me, an' if yer prepared to work ye can move mountains. The Harshaws taught me to read the Psalms; in one o' them it says: 'I to the hills will lift mine eyes, from whence shall come mine aid.' Just look at these mighty hills; never forget them Alice; if we always keep our eyes on them we'll never go wrong. We'll start in a small way: a few hens and geese maybe, a cow or two; as long as we can feed and clothe outselves we'll be all right. Next we'll get a field, then two fields, and by and by we'll have a farm. We'll make drains, build walls, and make roads. All the time we'll be rearin' a family: soon they'll be buildin' the walls and makin' the roads; an' . . . an' . . . mebbe one or two o' them might become teachers, preachers, or doctors an' do somethin' great in the world. Ye never can tell—when two people like us start out on the road o' life with our eyes on the hills, we're bound to end up higher than where we started."

During this speech Alice's eyes never left the face of the man she loved. She knew now beyond the shadow of a doubt that, come what may, the two of them together would win through. As the red sun began to slip behind Clermont Carn they came down from the Cloghmore Stone, now transformed and transfigured by the sun's glow.

Soon, all too soon, the honeymoon was over. On this last day they made an early start. Just before setting out there was the usual contretemps, or as Hugh was to say afterwards, a *schimozzelum*—the first discomfiture that most young husbands experience: when he went to pay his bill he found that, with complete disregard for money's ephemeral qualities, he hadn't a cent. Fortunately, however, Alice, anticipating just such a difficulty, had concealed about her person a bag containing the egg money which she tactfully slipped over to Hugh at the right moment.

They decided to walk along the white, whin-gilded road to Newry. In this dirty town, with its proud people, high church, and low steeple, they purchased presents for the priest, Paddy and Mr. Burns; then in a hired gig they were soon jogging along the tree-curtained lanes leading to Ballynaskeagh. As they came nearer the old home, two hearts accelerated slightly. What kind of welcome would be awaiting them ? This was the question in the minds of both.

Their worries were soon dispelled; no sooner did their horse come to a stop than the door was flung open, and there was Paddy, kind and impetuous as ever.

" Man Ah'm glad to see yez ! Alice ! " and he flung his arms around her; " Hugh ! welcome home ! " he gave Hugh's hand such a clasp in his great mutton fist that the aforesaid gentleman had perforce to separate each individual finger.

" This calls for a celebration ! Hie there you ! " he shouted to the girl, " out with thon bottle from the cupboard under the dresser ! Yez'll be cowld afther yer journey: we'll make a drop o' punch ! "

Though neither Hugh nor Alice were drinkers, as this was a very special occasion, what could they do other than accept Paddy's generosity ? And so in a few minutes the three of them, glad to be in each other's friendly company once more, were enjoying, not only the warmth engendered by the warm spirit, but also the warmth of Paddy's welcome.

" Man thon was the quare surprise ye sprang on us on the day o' the weddin'. But ye know Ah never felt really happy about the thought o' Alice marryin' Burns—a fine fella though, Ah'll say that for him—but too ould for our Alice. An' another thing: Ah felt all the time Ah was lettin' down the one really good friend Ah had in the world. It all goes to show that when ye have to choose between the heart an' the head, let the heart have its way."

" How did they take it ? " said Alice.

" How did they take it, sister dear ? Well Ah'll tell ye. By yer precipitate action the two o' yez done more good here to our wee community than was ever done by preacher or teacher. Ye brought us together around hearth and hearthstone in a way that people ought to be livin' together, instead o' listening to some o' thon rantin' politicians who are never happy unless they are separatin' people an' makin' them unhappy.

"An' there's sumpin' else Ah'm goin' to tell yez. Ye owe an awful lot to the Father. For a time it looked as if there might be trouble, but after he'd spoken there was hardly one wi' a dry eye in his head—a great man, a great man if iver there was one ! He had a good word for the two o' yez. He spoke o' yer love for each other; he spoke of your courage an' good faith; an' he said it didn't matther a damn whether yez were Catholics or Protestants as long as ye were good people an' loved each other for life.

" When he sat down everybody rose like one man, they drank to your health and happiness, an' they cheered yez 'till Ah thought they'd be heard in Banbridge. Ah'm tellin' ye no lies ! "

" An'—an'—there's just one other thing," continued Paddy as the fanned wrinkles of the fresh-air man folded at the corners of his eyes. " He said he hoped there'd be lots o' wee Brontës comin' to help wi' the farm; an' mebbe there might be one or two for the Church as well."

" How did Burns take it ? " Hugh said.

" Well now, what could ye expect ? " was the reply. " O' course he was disappointed. Who wouldn't 'a been at missin' a girl like our Alice. But Burns wasn't the kind o' man to get cross like; an' him havin' been wi'out a wumman

K

for so long, he mebbe began to think that it mightn't 'a been such a good idea after all to change his state so quickly. Anyhow the priest was gran' the way he talked to him; an' he towl him about a tidy wee woman wi' a good farm o' lan' marchin' on his. He as much as said he might be able to put in a word for him."

" An' how were things below at the Point ? "

Alice and Hugh just looked at each other and smiled. In spite of Hugh's gift for words, on this occasion he could find no words. How could he express the inexpressible ? Their experiences at the Point were in their own hearts and minds and bodies: all that had happened there was sacred and secret: it was something between themselves never to be shared with a living soul.

" Right ! Well yez 'ill be stayin' here the night anyhow ? "

Hugh and Alice smiled acquiescence for they had no other place to go.

" Good ! We'll get a few friends in an' make a night o' it. It'll make up a bit for the disappointment about the weddin'. We'll have some fiddlin' and singin', an' mebbe a dance or two. They'll all be dyin' to see yez; an' the sooner ye see them the bether. How about it ? "

Once again what could the pair of them say ? Perhaps they would rather have spent the evening quietly, but they didn't wish to spoil Paddy's fun. Anyhow they were still young; the prospect of a bit of a hooley was not without its attractions.

And it was a bit of a hooley and no mistake. Everybody seemed to know there was to be a *carry-on*. Fiddlers, whistlers, fluters, and fools appeared as if conjured out of the earth by a fairy wand. Reels, jigs, and hornpipes were danced with a lightness of heel-tapping, and a grace of leg-lifting that would have seemed impossible from those whose loins and limbs were more conditioned to the heavy-footed work of byre and barnyard, field and farmyard.

It is true that the pop songs of to-day become the folk songs of to-morrow. There was a song of those days: one that was becoming increasingly popular; it was to remain popular for centuries. And why not? With its charming words and lilting air. One feels it was sung at this party; for no song could have been more appropriate:

> Near to Banbridge town in the County Down
> On a morning in July,
> Down a boreen green came a sweet caileen,
> And she smiled as she passed me by.

Could there have been a more appropriate hero for the song than handsome Hugh, or a lovelier caileen than his darling Alice?

Of course the pair had to be toasted again and again. When Hugh was called on for a speech he fairly trembled, but taking a deep breath and squaring his shoulders he faced his audience with courage, and with wit and an easy flow of words that surprised not only his listeners, but also himself. He said in effect:

" Friends the last time we met Ah could hardly have called ye friends; but now all that's been forgotten; an' Ah just want to thank ye for the reception ye've given us here to-night.

" Ah may not be much o' a scholar—though thanks to the Harshaws and Alice Ah'm improvin' a bit in that respect—but there's some things Ah do know: Ah know the right end o' a cow; Ah know the difference between a stone an' a lump o' limestone; an' the difference between a well-built wall an' a bad 'un.

" An'—an' this was what Ah was comin' to—Ah also know the difference between a good-lookin' good girl, a good-lookin' bad girl, and a bad-lookin' good girl. When Ah saw Alice for the first time here in the doorway of this very house, Ah knew at once which she was; an' Ah fell in love with her straight away. As ye'll all admit, she's a lovely lookin' good girl. She's ' The Star o' the County Down.' If Ah could write a poem about her Ah'd say that she had eyes like stars, an' lips redder than Mars.

" Ah know we shouldn't have run away the way we did; but what else could we 'a done ? Now that we're back Ah'd just like to say that Alice and me want to make our livelihood here, an' live here for the rest o' our lives."

When Hugh sat down Alice felt proud of him; she knew now that they were fully accepted back into the hearts of the people she loved, and with whom she had grown up. But they hadn't been sitting very long before they were pulled to their feet while the whole company circled around them singing whatever was the eighteenth-century equivalent of " For They are Jolly Good Fellows."

CHAPTER 15

PATRICK'S NIGHT

HUGH'S head seemed scarcely to have touched the pillow that night when he heard Paddy's quiet knock at the bedroom door, while his voice informed him that Alice's mare was already saddled and bridled; and all was ready for him to make the dawn ride to Loughorne.

Giving Alice a farewell kiss, he told her that he would come over as often as possible; but because of calvings, lambings, and farrowings, he would have to remain above most nights. He was sure, however, that, when there were no special duties the Harshaws, very kindly and considerate people, would allow him to stay at home now and again. " Mebbe by the time Ah get back ye'll have a wee house all ready for us ! "

A characteristic of the County Down is—or used to be— that if local people get to know that you are coming to live in the district, everybody will go out of his or her way to try to find a suitable house for you, often to the extent of competing with each other in the house-hunting process. Whether or not this happened in this case is not known; eventually, however, a cottage was found in Emdale, or Imdell, just over the cross-roads as you proceed past the house at Ballynaskeagh in the direction of Loughbrickland to Rathfriland.

And what a house ! A shelter might be a better description: a mud-walled thatched cottage with a bare two rooms, neither more nor less: a peasant cottage of the lowest degree. There must have been hundreds of them in those days—there still are, though not many are now inhabited. The occupants lived, cooked, and worked in one room and slept in the other.

So when Hugh had completed his term with the Harshaws of Loughorne, this was the house in which he and Alice first settled down. Here it was they were to continue the early transports of their love life; and here it was that they began slowly but surely to build, stone upon stone, the edifice of their successful rural life. The simplest " two up and two down " would have been a palace by comparison.

It is hard to believe that any pair could have lived under such conditions without becoming roughened and brutalized, yet there is no evidence that this happened—quite the reverse in fact. The battles, blows, and barbarities of one sort or another, which have so often been the outward manifestations of the inward frustrations of those who have been held under the soul-destroying bondage of such poor dwellings, did not occur in their case.

Literally and metaphorically their eyes were always on the hills. Over the tumbling, rolling, coiling, and uncoiling hills of Down they could see away, away, to their beloved Mountains of Mourne on which they first saw their vision of what life could mean. Everlasting love in a cottage is possible, for there is always room outside, but there is not much room at the top of an urban tenement. It was said of Alice in after years that when she looked at Hugh, she never did so with a frown. Incredible ! maybe; but the fact that this was the legend supports its truth, for the evil that men do, or women for that matter, so often lives after them. Gossip is rarely good, especially about those who have stepped beyond the pale of convention: those who have been out of step, or have not toed the party line.

How did they live ? Very simply: money at first had no part in their way of life. Existence was all they lived for: food, clothing. We'll make our own food; we'll make our own clothing; this was the simple answer.

Apart from farming, Hugh had no manual skills. He couldn't farm; he had no cash with which to buy either land or stock, and he would have required both. He couldn't cobble for either horses or men; he could neither join nor build, for he was neither a joiner nor a builder. He was determined to be independent. What then could he do ? He could dry grain for the flour mill; and as a reward he would be allowed to keep some of the grain for himself; this the miller would grind for him on payment of some of his own allowance to the miller. They could bake flour with the bread.

What more would they need ? eggs, milk, potatoes. Paddy, out of the kindness of his heart, allowed them a rood of his land on which to grow potatoes. A few hens and maybe a stripper cow were sufficient to give them enough eggs and milk in the meantime. No Irish cottage, however mean or humble, would have been complete without the odd pig poking about in the fields and furrows for anything it could pick up, or nosing among old pots and pans for the remains of porridge and potatoes.

Alice, skilled in the art of spinning, kept a couple of sheep, the wool from which provided her with yarn. How did she dye the yarn ? This is not recorded but surely natural dyes would have been available in a countryside dyed blue, red, and purple each autumn. Anyhow with the coloured yarn she knitted—yes, knitted !—clothes for herself and Hugh, and later for her rapidly growing family.

So, while Hugh sat in front of his tiny corn kiln with his heap of shelled corn beside him, Alice sang to the rhythm of her spinning wheel. At least they were warm ! The whole process of the drying was almost self-generating, and it was certainly economical for the corn shells provided re-fuelling for the fire, heat for the house, and a red glow of light. Thus Alice and Hugh lived the good life, which so many in our day and generation have sought after. *They* did it out of necessity, unlike the drop-outs of our day who do it to rid themselves of the restrictions, frustrations, uncertainties, and instabilities of our modern existence.

Out of all the fact, fiction, stories false and stories true extant at the time and later, the incredible emerges: Alice retained her beauty and they both retained love from the beginning of their lives together until the end. The poem below, of which a hint was given earlier, was supposed to have been written by Hugh. Some think that he, though he appears to have had some natural and acquired ability in the shaping of words, could scarcely have produced a poem of such obvious merit. Though the poem may have been polished by their son Patrick, the sentiments must have been there; and indeed its construction, alliteration, rhythm, and music show little in common with Patrick's published poems.

ALICE AND HUGH

The red rose paled before the blush
    That mantled o'er thy dimpled cheek;
The fresh bloom faded at the flush
    That tinged thy beauty ripe and meek.

Thy milk-white brow outshone the snow,
    Thy lustrous eyes out-glanced the stars;
Thy cherry lips with love aglow
    Burned redder than the blood-red Mars.

Thy sweet, low voice waked in my heart
    Dead memories of my mother's love;
My long lost sister's artless art
    Lived in thy smiles, my gentle dove.

Dear Alice, how thy charm and grace
    Kindled my dull and stagnant life !
From first I saw they winning face
    My whole heart claimed thee for my wife.

I thought you'd make me happy, dear,
    I sought you for my very own;
You clung to me through storm and fear,
    You loved me still, though poor and lone.

My love was centred all in self,
  Thy love was centred all in me;
True love above all pride and pelf,
  My life's deep current flows for thee.

The finest fibres of my soul
  Entwine with thine in love's strong fold,
Our tin cup is a golden bowl,
  Love fills our cot with wealth untold.

Not long after the two had settled into their tiny home
Hugh noticed that Alice wasn't quite herself. Though she
complained little it was obvious that something was limiting
her usual vitality. Occasionally her breakfast was untouched;
jobs that caused her no difficulty before now seemed too
much for her.

"What ails ye, Alice ?" Hugh said one day.

"Ah don't know, Hugh, but Ah don't seem to be up to
things somehow."

"Mebbe the place is too small; perhaps we should look for
a bigger house. There's one over there at Lisnacreevy that
Ah've had me eye on for some time."

"Not at all, Hugh dear. Ah'll be all right when the spring
comes, don't you worry."

But the feeling of sickness was soon to disappear, and Alice
was her own self once more. One day, while singing merrily
at the spinning wheel, with Hugh beside her in the kiln's glow,
she bent down, drew his head to her lap and said:

"Hugh, there's somethin' Ah want to tell ye !"

"What is it, mavourneen ?" he answered, using a term
of endearment he remembered from his Boyne days.

"Ah'm goin' to have a baby !"

How often had this same statement been made before ?
How often had it been greeted with chagrin, sorrow, fear,
joy ? This time it was joy unmistakable.

Suddenly Hugh jumped to his feat, nearly knocking the bars from his miniature corn kiln, and shouted so that he could have been heard from Emdale to Ballynaskeagh and beyond:

" A baby ! A baby ! A Brontë baby ! Yippee ! Oh, Alice." He swept her from his stool and hugged her until she began to fear for the infant within her body.

" Easy ! easy ! me darlin' man, Ah do want to have the baby ye know."

The remaining months before the big event passed happily. Hugh went about his daily chores with excitement and happiness in his heart. Like most other farming men he hoped for a boy as his first-born, but he would be happy either way, for a girl like Alice would have been equally acceptable. Alice, after her first set-back, like many another peasant woman, was able to work almost up to the day when the birth seemed imminent.

The long, hard winter was gradually giving place to spring's gentle invasion. Buds and early blossoms began to test the air to see if it was time for the perennial resurrection. One day Red Paddy said:

" As soon as Saint Patrick turns the warm side o' the stone up, we'll have to be soddin' the spuds." And then he added with a wink:

" But mebbe by that time ye'll have other things on yer mind ! "

When Saint Patrick turned up the warm side of the stone on the 17th March, 1777, baby Patrick Brontë also joined in the pæon of praise in anticipation of spring's perennial resurrection.

CHAPTER 16

NATURE'S GENTLEMAN

ONE might well ask how a child could be brought up in such circumstances. What with the smoke, smells, dirt, and damp, one would be inclined to think that such an environment would be a killer for any child, strong or otherwise. But there are probably more children killed by cold, damp, malnutrition, disease germs, and traffic than in any other way; and of course the presence of all of these adverse conditions at once tends to promote a dangerous vicious cycle.

However, a second glance at the Brontë way of life at this time discloses the fact that all of these conditions were not present, or at least they were modified by the rural way of living. Whatever else one might say about the cottage, it certainly would not have been cold; and because it was not cold neither was it damp. Even if there were, at times, limitations to the flow of air within, there certainly was no limitation outside where the air extended to the widest limits in every direction, both upwards and outwards. Contact with disease germs grows in direct proportion to contact with other human beings; and, as the Brontës rarely had any associations with pubs, clubs, dance halls, or even churches, their germ intake was probably limited. Milk would have been a hazard, but fresh air and some degree of immunization may have prevented them from becoming a prey to the chief scourge of the times.

As to nutrition: milk, eggs, spuds, butter, bread—not much variety; but along with clear sunshine through unadulterated air, is there any other essential requirement for a growing child? And with the trafficless lanes and roads around Emdale, there was no need for the mother's constant frightened cry of " Come on out o' that ! "—a cry so trying for the nerves of both mother and child.

Thus Patrick Brontë's early days may not have been so adverse to his physical and mental growth as some biographers have been wont to indicate. As he began to toddle about, too, he would have had the loving care and attention of parents who were always around; and there would have been lots of things in which to be interested: horses, cows, dogs, pigs, with all their attendant noises; and just across the land there was a spreading tree with a smithy underneath. Here the toddler would be safe under the smith's watchful eye; and here too he would have been fascinated by the fireworks display as the showers of star-like sparks flew upwards from the roaring bellows.

However, the most of Patrick's toddling was done, not from the tiny cottage at Emdale, but from a more commodious dwelling in Lisnacreevy, about half a mile away. When Alice realized, toward the end of the ensuing year, that she was again pregnant, Hugh said:

" We'll have to get a bigger place; this was right enough when there was only you and me; but it'll not do for a large family. We can afford more than a tanner a week now. Besides, Ah can get plenty o' work apart from the corn dryin'. Ah'll tell ye what Ah'll take a run over an' have a look at thon house at Lisnacreevy Ah was tellin' ye about."

" Whatever ye say, Hugh, we certainly couldn't go on livin' here as things are. An' it would be better for you to be movin' about more instead o' bein' bent over the kiln all day, an' half the night."

" Right ye be," replied Hugh, " as soon as Ah get redd up here Ah'll go over; Ah'll find out who's the agent an' get everything fixed up. Paddy 'll lend us the horse and cart, mebbe we could be in by to-morrow."

" There ye go ! always wantin' to put the cart before the horse; yer in far too big a hurry, man. The place 'll have to be cleaned up first; an' mebbe the walls 'll have to be papered an' one thing an' another."

True to his word, as soon as the poultry and pigs had been fed, Hugh cleaned himself up and stepped down to Paddy, who was hard at it cleaning a drain in one of his nearby fields.

" Could ye give us the loan o' a horse, Pat ? Ah want to have a look at the vacant place down the road at Lisnacreevy; an' then mebbe Ah'll have a word with the agent."

" A gran' idea, man, Ah never liked to say it till yez 'cause it wasn't my business, but thon place is far too small. Wee Pat 'ud need a bit more room now that he's beginnin' to trot around. How's he doin' ? "

" How's he doin' ? Man, sure he's makin' rings around him; he's a gran' wee fella. Before long he'll be over here givin' ye a bit o' a hand about the place."

" Good ! Away along with ye now an' the best o' luck. The mare's as fresh as paint—plenty o' good oats. Ye'll need to keep a tight rein on her."

Hugh was soon in the saddle. First of all he trotted around the corner to have a look at the house which was approached by a lane leading some distance into the fields back from the road. Being a countryman he instinctively noticed the land and the directions. " Good farmin' land—the very best," he thought. Away to the south-east the terrain undulated quietly until it reached the blue dimly seen hills of the Mournes. In the adjacent quarter to the south-west lay Newry, and further west, Poyntzpass. According to his reckoning Banbridge lay almost due north.

The house was in fair condition. " A bit o' paint and lime here and there," he thought. But he knew that between the two of them they could cope with anything; and so, nothing daunted, he soon found the big house where, after a little haggling, he made his bargain with the agent, then went back to Alice to tell her the good news, and to look again at the miracle of his first-born of whom he couldn't see enough.

A few days later their few belongings, amounting to the bed and cot, two or three chairs, a table of sorts, and their pots and pans, were piled on Red Paddy's cart, and they were away without tears. Without tears, yes, but not without a little sentiment. After all this had been their first nest; they had made love together here; and this was where the boy, on whom they now pinned such high hopes, had been born on that auspicious day, 17th March, 1777.

Soon they were in the home that was to be theirs for the next sixteen years, during which all their children, save one—the youngest, Alice—were to be born. It was far from being a big house, but it appears to have been adequate. Though the rent was higher Hugh seemed to have little difficulty in meeting his commitments. Not only did he continue with the corn-drying, but he was able to add cash to his payments in kind by the profitable and satisfying task of fence-making and road repairing.

Thus it came about that, in a country where money was normally scarce and living cheap, Hugh, like many another for whom work was habitual and almost perpetual, had little trouble in making enough in money and kind to provide for the needs of his growing family, or a family that was soon to grow both in numbers and in stature.

Not only did the family grow, but Hugh also grew intellectually and socially. Neighbours and friends would often call in at night to hear Hugh talk. He could tell stories with such dramatic power that he came to believe in them; and what is more, he often sent his listeners home in a state of terror.

" Come on now, Hugh," a neighbour would say as the circle around the fire widened, " give us a bit o' yer ould crack ! "

And Hugh rarely disappointed, though sometimes when not in the mood for story-telling, he would instead become political; and he would advance his theories on the rights of man, particularly the rights of those who were tenants in a country where the tenant had few rights.

Much that he is reported to have said then has now become axiomatic. Much that he said then gave rise to ideas which, in their turn, led to the rising of the United Irishmen in 1798, and to that of the Young Irishmen in 1848. And indeed, if he did express such ideas he must have been an uneducated man with a high degree of intelligence.

His propositions were well thought out and well presented. Briefly, he was " agin " the establishment: you did not give allegiance to either Church or State when both ignored, and sometimes even supported injustice; a king was wrong who turned a blind eye on the poverty of his subjects; the lords of the land and all their minions were wrong when they allowed their land to fall into decay, and housed their tenants in hovels; a church that supported lucrative landlords, and did nothing to alleviate the poverty-stricken peasantry was not fulfilling its obligations; a church that kept its people in a state of suppression, ignorance and superstition was in opposition to its professed beliefs. Improvements to lands and houses should be used for the benefit of those who made the improvements. He was no believer in a God who appeared to be on the side of those who perpetrated injustice.

Such pebbles dropped into the waters of local thought must have caused waves to go out, which may have had a considerable influence at a time when evolution and revolution were very much in mind and action. As we saw earlier, not only did the Harshaws influence Hugh, but Hugh's story also had an influence on the Harshaws. And it was inevitable that such ideas must have gone deeply into the minds of Hugh's sons, one of whom was later to become a United Irishman; he fought at the Battle of Ballynahinch.

One doesn't know how, where, or when Alice was educated, for at the time when she was young the education of Catholics, save at the Hedge Schools, would have presented difficulties. It seems likely that Alice was the inspiration of Hugh's earlier attempts at reading, just as the younger Cathy helped the neglected Hareton Earnshaw to pull himself out of the slough of ignorance into which he had been thrust by Heathcliffe.

The household library consisted of four books: Alice's New Testament, Hugh's Bible, *Pilgrim's Progress,* and a copy of *The Works of Robert Burns.* Four well-thumbed books: how often have these four had an incalculable effect on the semi-literate minds of their readers ?

CHAPTER 17

LINEN AND LITERATURE

WHATEVER may have been the influence of these four books on Hugh and Alice, they certainly were to penetrate into the conscious and unconscious mind of the eldest son Patrick, who was now growing up to be a particularly handsome and striking-looking lad: crisp reddish hair, an aquiline nose, and eyes of the watery blue which so often goes with red or dark hair in Ireland; eyes which could suddenly become fierce and penetrating.

Patrick's imagination was also fired by his father's tales of his early life, by his telling of folk-tales, and stories that appeared to well up in him like the bubbling waters of a local spring. " Tell us a story, Papa," would often be the evening's entertainment in the firelight glow, in much the same way as the modern child would obtain his by switching on the radio or television. Many children nowadays are bored by parental stories. This was not always the case, and certainly it was not so in the days before television began to dominate the family scene. Decades ago, especially in the country, many a small boy would sit quietly entranced in a hard chair with his feet dangling, while his father told some hair-raising tale of long ago, when he was a boy.

And as Patrick grew so did the family: about every two years or so there would be a new brother until there were five boys in all; and then as though nature had—in local parlance— " caught herself on " there were five sisters at the same intervals of time except once, when two arrived at the same time. All lived to a great old age, save one of the girls who was to die in her thirties. The children were: William, who followed Patrick in 1779, he lived to be eighty-three; Hugh, born in 1781, lived to be eighty-two; then came James in 1783, he reached eighty-seven; Walsh, 1786, was eighty-two when he died. Jane, born in 1789, was the only one to die young—in her thirties; the twins, Rose and Sara, were born in 1793; Rose died when she was seventy-seven, and Sara at eighty-two—pretty good for twins ! All of these, with the exception of Patrick, were born at the Lisnacreevy home; Alice, the youngest, was born at the final home at Ballynaskeagh—she was to reach the ripe old age of ninety-seven.

An excellent record when one considers the hazards to life in those days; and a wonderful advertisment for their way of living which was of the simplest: breakfast—porridge and milk; dinner—spuds in their skins; piece-time—home-made bread with buttermilk; supper—potatoes, boiled milk, occasionally an egg. The bread was mostly potato-bread or fadge made with oatmeal—good enough in restricted quantity but as a filler reputed to incite heartburn. It is sometimes stated that Patrick's chronic indigestion was caused by a surfeit of his mother's bread, but it could just as easily have been produced by his scholarly way of life; indeed it might almost be described as scholar's disease !

And so, inwardly warmed by fadge, and sowans—a kind of oatmeal jellied soup—and outwardly warmed by their characteristic woollen, Alice-spun, and Alice-knitted garments, is it any wonder that this partially ostracized family of a mixed marriage grew up to be individualists and eccentrics ? Apart from the necessity for obtaining the maximum amount of heat from materials available on a limited purse, it seems that Hugh's obsessional dread of fire, which was to be passed on to Patrick, made the wearing of wool preferable to the wearing of cotton or linen.

With a good-looking mother—a local beauty—and a handsome father, was it any wonder that the genetic link producing good looks was transmitted to the family ? It is reported that the men were all tall, and of striking appearance, while the sisters were tall, red-cheeked, fair-haired and hand-some, with dark eyelashes, *strong minds and massive frames*. Possibly the emphasized part of this description explains why only one, Sara, married and mothered ten children.

Thus Patrick, whatever else he may have been, was certainly not at any time an only spoiled child. As soon as he was capable of it, he would have been expected to gather eggs, gather sticks, bring in turf for the fire, feed the hens, and in general help with the household chores. There were sights, sounds and smells to which his sensitive nature would have to become inured, for example, the squeals of a stuck pig, or the killing of a hen by the simple process of removing its neck with a sharp knife. Other boys around the country would probably call out with boyish cruelty: " papish bastard," " to hell with the Pope," and other insulting references to his mixed origin.

The killing of a pig was welcomed because it meant more substantial fare for some time to come: all sorts of dainties would be extracted from it—bacon, brains, and brawn, and lard for frying. Occasionally Paddy would slaughter a cow or a bull that had completed its living function. This usually happened at festival times: Christmas, Easter, Hallowe'en; then they would have the luxury of " butcher's meat."

" Away ye go now an' bring in a lock o' peppermint and horehound for the tea makin' ! " Alice would say.

The order was important for the beverage was greatly prized when few beverages other than milk were available. There was a time when a worker wouldn't work without his guaranteed peppermint tea. It must have been something of a luxury, for an addicted girl could be an unmarriageable girl: she would be too extravagant ! The plants, when gathered, would be hung in a loft to dry; when infused later, not only did they provide a beverage but also an antidote for the water-brash (heartburn). The tea was taken with milk and sugar.

In those days a " barefoot " boy was commoner than a shod one. Patrick was probably a teenager before he knew what it felt like to wear a pair of boots.

" Right, boys, we're out for the spud gatherin' to-day ! " was a dreadful order; for the back-breaking, soul-destroying job had little of the harmonious joy of harvest days in sun-filled fields. Usually the work had to be done barefooted on cold, damp earth under a wetting continual drizzle. And you had to work like the " hammers o' hell " to keep your man or two men going with his " diggin' grape." Even with mechanical diggers the job can be hard, for you have to lift into the baskets without respite to keep the digger going on each run; but when a barefooted child had to pull at the stalks to clear them and help the digging man, it was indeed an unenviable task; and one calculated to cause pain and sometimes bleeding.

While Patrick, and the other boys, had little stomach for the digging, Patrick certainly liked the forge: he haunted it. He loved the upward leaping sparks, the warmth, and the roaring rush of the hand-heaved bellows; and he liked also the warm, sweet smell of hot iron being pressed home to the yielding hoof of a hard-working horse. Since he was so fond of the forge, was it any wonder that he was soon to become the blacksmith's assistant ?

A passing horseman of good address and demeanour drew up at the Emdale forge one day to have his horse shod.

" Can you shoe my horse, blacksmith ? " he said.

" Aye, o' coorse," replied the blacksmith, " Ah could hardly refuse a gentleman like yourself."

" A gentleman ! " the client retorted. " How do you know I'm a gentleman ? "

" Ah can tell be the looks o' ye. It's only a gentleman could afford clothes like yours; an' look at thon saddle an' bridle—ye didn't get them for nothin' ! "

" So you think it's the money and the clothes that makes a gentleman ?"

" Och well now Ah wouldn't go as far as to say that, Ah suppose it's sumpin' in the way a man treats ye."

" His manners you mean ? "

" Aye, Ah suppose ye could call it that. If Ah might ask, Sir, can you, as a man with some education, tell *me* what makes a gentleman ? "

The stranger considered the point for a few seconds; and then he said:

" In my humble opinion there are three kinds of gentlemen: gentlemen by birth, gentlemen by fortune, and gentlemen by nature. Now, do you see that young lad there ? " he continued in raised tones. " That young lad is obviously a gentleman by nature."

From that day until the day of his death Patrick never forgot this. It was to be a lodestone to his life from then on to the extent that on his eighty-second birthday he is reported to have informed Mr. John Greenwood, the local stationer at Haworth, that " No one could tell what effect these few words had upon me through life." Mr. Greenwood, recording the incident in his diary, added his own comment: " How true and how prophetic were the words of this poor blacksmith ! How oft have *we* had to remark that he was a real, a thorough gentleman." What a difference the right word at the right time can make to a person's whole life !

But books, books, and more books were soon to become Patrick's chief obsession. Did he teach himself to read ? It would appear to be so, for he certainly had read his father's books before being formally educated. Limited reading, you might say, and you would be right: true education, however, does not consist in the number of books one reads, but in the quality of those books, and the extent to which they have made an impression on the mind. So at night, while others talked, Patrick would be quiet in the fire glow in a world of *Pilgrim's Progress*.

Though Hugh and Alice made no attempt to discourage Patrick in his reading, because of the growing family, the earning of his living became a matter of serious importance; and in a land where the weaving of fine linen was becoming an increasingly lucrative business, it became obvious that the weaving of linen, fine or otherwise, would be a suitable trade for a young fellow. Accordingly he was apprenticed to a local weaver, a Mr. Donald.

Not only did this provide him with a skilled occupation, and money in his pocket, but it also gave him book-hunting opportunities, because he was often sent with wefts of brown linen to the brown-linen markets in Banbridge and Newry. Here he could browse among books wherever and whenever book stalls were there for the browsing.

And he was actually sent to Belfast. He had money in his pocket when he set out; when he returned he had none. Was it a case of Goldsmith's Moses returning from the fair? No! When Patrick returned he had something much more valuable than a gross of the green spectacles: he had a gross of books which were to give him profit, pleasure, and inspiration for months to come. Now, instead of just weaving monotonously, he could weave harmoniously and joyfully as the words of Milton's "Paradise Lost" became his paradise, and the wefts ran out from the clicking loom.

Just as his father's love-life caused deterioration of his work at the Mount Pleasant lime kiln, so Patrick's love of books was to cause a falling-off in his weaving efficiency. Consequently Mr. Donald had no great objections to a transfer to a Mr. Clibborn of Banbridge; a man who had been an admirer of Hugh's work. But Mr. Clibborn required linen of the finest texture, and was disappointed when he found that one of Patrick's wefts was not up to standard; a mind divided between linen and "Paradise Lost" was incapable of rendering unto both maximum concentration.

Then a miracle happened: it was to change the course of his life. On a lovely day in that lovely land Patrick was in his favourite private place, Emdale Fort. With no one in sight, as he thought, but in full view of the Mourne Mountains, he was pacing up and down, his Milton in front of him, reciting with his arms gesticulating to high heaven such measures as

High on a throne of royal state, which far
Outshone the wealth of Ormus and of Ind,
Or where the gorgeous East with richest hand
Showers on her king a barbaric pearl and gold,

. . . .

Then much to his chagrin, and with reddening face, he heard a gentle cultured voice saying:

" Well young man, what are you up to ? "

" Reading Milton," said the discomfited Patrick.

" Reading Milton ! That's an unusual occupation for a young fellow. Here, now, let's see ! " and the gentleman gave Hugh line for line; in no time they were discussing Milton together; and soon this " stickit " Presbyterian school-master, Rev. Andrew Harshaw, and Patrick, were friends.

Harshaw was an outstanding classical and mathematical scholar who, lacking success as a minister, had become the one teacher of the one-teacher school at Ballynafern. People in those days expected volume more than value; if a minister couldn't speak for an hour or two with " nothin' in his han'," his hearers didn't think much of him. Harshaw was too much of a thinker to speak without thought; thus, being no exponent of empty oratory, he remained a minister without a congrega-tion—a *stickit* minister.

But he must have been a born teacher, for the hall-mark of the good teacher is one who is quick to recognize merit in others; and is more interested in the success of his pupils than in his own success.

" What do you do for a living ? " Harshaw enquired of the fifteen-year-old Patrick.

" I'm a linen weaver but . . ."

" But what ? "

" Well I'd like to have more time for books and learning; and I'd like to be something better. Linen weaving is all right; the wages are good, but you're doing the same thing all the time."

" What would you like to be ? "

" Oh, I don't know—a teacher, maybe; a minister, a poet or writer of some sort; but I don't see much hope."

" Well, I don't know; it's wonderful what you can do if you have a mind to it."

Suddenly Harshaw was inspired to an idea. He felt that he himself was something of a failure; he had never been able to realize his full potential. Teaching small kids " the three R's " wasn't enough, but here was a boy that he might be able to inspire to greatness.

" Tell me," he said after some thought, " at what time do you start work in the morning ? "

" I generally leave at dawn."

" Well, now, if you're really keen come over to my place a couple of hours before you leave, and I'll give you all the schooling I can."

" Oh, sir, would you really ! Why that would be wonderful," Patrick said, his voice full of scarcely suppressed excitement.

And so it came about that Patrick, with but four to five hours' sleep behind him, would go over to Harshaw's bedroom every morning to be taught by the bed-reclining minister for two hours before he began his walk—the five-mile walk to distant Banbridge. His eyes overstrained by weaving linen all day would be further over-strained by weaving the fabric of mathematics and the classics at night.

Fortunately, before his eyes were irreparably damaged, his Banbridge boss died; as he had now no other occupation, he had a good excuse for becoming a full-time scholar, in the hope that he would soon have sufficient qualifications to enable him to apply for a teaching post.

His ambitions were soon to be realized; a teacher was required for the nearby Presbyterian Church School at Glasgar; Brontë applied under the sponsorship of Harshaw, but he was at first turned down on the grounds that his mother

Glasgar School.

The Brown Linen Market and the Bunch of Grapes in Old Banbridge—1783.

was a Catholic. The appointed candidate, however, refused the offer with the result that the Church authority had no option; and so Patrick was appointed.

And from the age of sixteen, for five years, he was to make an excellent and a most progressive teacher. How many of his contemporaries at that time would have refused to use either rod or tawse? How many would have taken the trouble to find out the abilities of each boy and girl under their care, so that they could teach them accordingly? How many would have made a point of discussing each pupil's progress, or lack of it, with the parents concerned? And how many would have taken their pupils out into the highways and by-ways to study nature and local geography? Precious few, one would surmise! When you add to all this the fact that he brought the slower pupils back in the evening for further tuition, you will agree that here was a teacher of unusual calibre.

Though religious observance had not so far played a big part in his life, he felt it his duty to attend the Church with which his school was associated, and so he was usually to be seen at church on Sunday. Not only was he to be seen at church, but he was also to take an active part in the service by training and conducting the small choir. In doing all this he was creating a pattern to be followed by many local school teachers for generations.

Patrick must also have been one of the few men of his profession at that time to take seriously the dictum, *mens sana in corpore sano*. He introduced gymnastics into his curriculum; and took his pupils on exploration trips even to the relatively far-away Mourne Mountains. Here they were introduced to that country's excellent botanical reservoir; and they were taught to appreciate the wondrous beauty of this gracious, granite pile. On one occasion, during a skating session on Loughorne, the ice began to rumble ominously; with considerable courage and coolness Patrick conducted his young charges across the ice to safety.

How did it happen that a boy—for he was little more—with no professional training in education—had sufficient knowledge to enable him to adopt such excellent educational methods ? One can find only one answer: Patrick Brontë was an inspired teacher.

There was another penetrating injection into Patrick's mind at this time or earlier. When a young boy with his uncluttered mind still open to conditioning influences, hears a powerful preacher proclaiming God's spell from the hill-tops, the effect can be everlasting. Wesley sustained two hopes: progress in the good life here, leading to the glory of a greater life beyond.

What an experience it must have been to see and hear this great man with his cultured voice, and arms pointing upward toward heavens that flamed with the light of the evening sun setting behind the hills of Down !

". . . . Protestants and Papists flocked together to the meadows where I preached and sat on the grass still as night while I exhorted them to repent and believe the Gospel."

This is an extract from Wesley's journal; the meadow was near Rathfriland.

And another extract reads as follows:

" But before we came to Loughbrickland my strength was so exhausted I was glad to stop at a little inn and send to Banbridge, about two miles off, for a post-chaise." The carriage in which Wesley was travelling from Rathfriland to Tandragee had broken down. Patrick had witnessed the incident. It is not surprising that he remained a Wesleyan, at least in outlook, to the end of his days.

Then came disaster—or near disaster. Like his father before him, he was to fall in love with the wrong girl at the wrong time, but with a difference: Hugh's wrong girl proved to be the right one for him, whereas Patrick's wrong girl was wrong for him. In what might be called a permissive, promiscuous age, neither Hugh nor Patrick were either, but they were precocious and romantic. Patrick's seductive red-haired Helen had neither Alice's constancy nor character, yet he loved her—or thought he lover her—romantically and physically.

He wrote poetry for her—at this time he was writing verse of sorts—and he kissed her in a hay-field behind a hay-stack.

Unfortunately, Helen's father, a man of substance, was one of the school managers; he didn't take kindly to an affair between his daughter—a fourteen-year-old pupil at the school—and the £40 a year schoolmaster, so Patrick was fired. Before this he was beaten up by some of the local boys who described him as a " mongrel papish bastard." The boys, having heard of the affair, were doubtless consumed with jealous hatred which they vented on the hapless Patrick.

Harshaw was extremely angry when he heard what had happened; he sent for Patrick. "Look, Patrick," he said, " I'm very annoyed and upset about this. I had great hopes for you; but now, through this foolish action, all my hopes have been dashed, and your life could very well be in a shambles. All our good work together has been set at nought."

Patrick reddened; and the veins stood out on his forehead; always liable to sudden outbursts, his lack of sufficient sleep and hard work had suddenly accelerated this tendency. So he retorted with some heat:

" I am fully conscious of all you've done for me, sir; but that doesn't give you the right to interfere in my private life."

" What you've done is inexcusable and childish. It's not just a matter of your private life; it's a matter of your public life and your relationship with your pupils. It's your public morals that have been called into question. Who is going to employ you now ? "

At length the justice of Harshaw's indignation began to seep through into Patrick's mind; and his good sense gained the upper hand. He regretted what he had said, and made genuine apology to his friend.

But the harm had been done. He had no recourse now other than to go back to following the plough with Red Paddy. Though he still continued to read, to write poetry, and to have romantic thoughts about Helen, his love was not reciprocated. The feckless, faithless Helen, no longer finding romance in the poet schoolmaster, now become poet peasant,

would have nothing further to do with him. What a difference
it might have made to life and literature if Patrick's suit had
been successful !

Fortunately the young man's foolish mistake was not to
follow him. Others had an eye on this exceptional teacher
who was too good to be wasted. In those days one often
hears a considerable amount of criticism of the Church and
its ministers of any denomination, especially in the country of
our present concern. They have often been accused of
perpetuating differences, or at the least of dragging their feet.
Sometimes the good has been too often interred with their
bones; we are inclined to forget all too easily how they have
been a lamp of learning in rural localities; and have often done
a great deal to inspire likely young people to aspire to higher
things, even to the extent of giving financial help from their
own, often meagre, purses.

Such an one was John Wesley's giant, Reverend Barber of
Rathfriland, who interested himself in Patrick; he introduced
him to, and often lent him, books from his own library,
including such famous works as Spenser's *Fœrie Queen*. But
the one who was to have the most profound influence was the
Rev. Thomas Tighe, Rector of Drumgooland; he had in his
charge the parish church of Drumballyroney which had a
small attached school without a teacher. At the same time the
Rector was looking for a suitable tutor for his children.

And who could be more suitable than Patrick ? An outstanding teacher with progressive views was exactly the type of
man Tighe wanted, both for the school and for his children.
The forbidden kiss had been forgotten, both in Tighe's mind
and in Patrick's. The post was accepted with alacrity; thus
Patrick was again to come under the influence of a scholar
with a fine library, and an admirer and friend of John Wesley,
who had often stayed with the family on his journeys.

The change from the Presbyterian Church to the Parish
Church meant little in a country where the churches were
usually low in their form of worship as well as in their
steeples. And here, too, at Rathfriland, Brontë's beloved

Mournes rose in a great high, solid billow from the valley between them and Rathfriland's drumlin, one of the biggest eggs in Down's basket of eggs.

At Drumballyroney school on a height overlooking Rathfriland, with the Mournes circling the background, Patrick taught with zeal and with the same progressive instinct as he had exercised to the full at Glasgar Hill. Many a time in later years, looking across from the hill-positioned Haworth, he must have called up happy memories of his Drumbally-roney days.

And they were happy days: so different from the peasant cottage and Lisnacreevy days of his earlier years. Living in the civilized surroundings of a country rectory with the great works of the masters of English literature at his disposal, was a new experience, especially for a man with his receptive mind. He, and his family, were all to become members of Drum-ballyroney Church; most of them are buried there, and there are existing baptismal records in the Parish Registers of Drumgooland. Here, too, the Wesleyan influence was to become even more deeply entrenched in his mind; and of a Sunday his full-throated baritone would be joined with the rude rural voices in the apt hymns of John and Charles Wesley.

" Lo, to faith's enlightened sight
 All the mountain flames with light; "

Three years had passed when once again Patrick's mind was to flame with a new light. With money from his public and private teaching in his pocket he began to wonder if . . . if. . . . And then one day Mr. Tighe, whose mind had been working in the same direction, called him into his study:

" Patrick" he said, " I have been wondering if you had given serious thought to the possibility of going to a university with a view to entering the Church ? "

Scarcely able to conceal the emotion from his voice, Patrick said:

" But do you think I'd be good enough, sir ? "

" Good enough ! How do you mean, good enough ? Do you mean in character or ability ? My dear chap, you're good enough in both. I just wish all our prospective candidates could measure up to your standards."

Patrick was overwhelmed—more so when he heard Mr. Tighe's next remark:

"Now as to the university, I would suggest Cambridge; I could get you accepted as a sizar at my old college, St. John's, where fees and living are reasonable. What do you think?"

"Cambridge! Cambridge!" thought Patrick, why this would exceed his wildest dreams. To go to Cambridge, that centuries-old centre of learning with its ancient colleges, its lawns, its traditions. To be a scholar of Cambridge; could anything be more wonderful? He had read about it; he had heard about it from Mr. Tighe, but to go there himself . . . the very thought made him breathless.

"I cannot think of anything I'd like better, sir," was all he could say.

"Right, well we'll start making arrangements immediately. You'll probably be able to pick up scholarships as you go along; these will help you to supplement your savings. Oh, and by the way, you needn't think that you'll be the only poor scholar. Most of us have found ourselves in the same boat. You'll find many others working their way through on meagre means. And another thing, the faculty of divinity is very strong at St. John's.

The upshot of all this was that in September, 1802, at the age of twenty-five, Patrick Brontë set sail for England with excitement in one corner of his heart at the prospects before him, and a desperate gnawing home-sickness in another corner as he watched the boat moving further and further from the misty Mourneland. As he gazed tears of both joy and sorrow mingled in his eyes; these were not the only tears he was to shed in the many years still to come.

From this time forth he was no longer a Brontë of Ballynaskeagh; he was to become a scholar of St. John's, an A.B. of Cambridge University, ultimately the imcumbent of the Parish of Haworth in Yorkshire and, above all, the father of Charlotte, Emily, and Anne, not forgetting, of course, Maria,

Elizabeth and Bramwell who, had it not been for the circumstance of their untimely death, might also have shown some measure of the family genius.

The journey alone in those days of sailing ships and coaches must have been something of an adventure. However, it was safely accomplished; and so with only his brains and £130 or so of his savings in his pocket, he was soon to present himself for registration at John's. When asked his name he said *Brontë* with a County Down accent. Accordingly the Registrar wrote down Branty, a mistake which was later corrected, at Patrick's request, by the college butler.

One can but dimly understand the feelings of this young man, raw from the scattered villages and hamlets of his native country, as he gazed at the colleges, heard the choirs, and saw the spires of this, to him, palatial university town. But he was not overawed; in spite of all his disadvantages of birth and upbringing, he was able to hold his own with the best, both socially and academically.

He was to win scholarships, prizes, and exhibitions to the extent that he became, not only financially independent, but also he was able to send home £20 a year to Alice, a practice he continued until the day of her death. Though he managed his affairs very well at all times, both as a student and later, he had to scrape the bottom of the barrel in order to find the wherewithal on which to live.

What did he leave to posterity ? Little, except his example of great courage in the face of adversity, suffering, frustration, and almost unendurable personal sorrow. He remained in the Wesleyan tradition, a great preacher whose sermons are still remembered in print. He wrote considerable quantities of poetry, the best known being his *Cottage Poems* which he may have written during his Glasgar days. He might have been a better poet had he written naturally rather than attempting a stilted classical style influenced by his scholarship. His somewhat banal novel, *Killarney,* is an interesting relic which gives a picture of the Irish life of his time.

M

Though he left little of literary value in his own right, he has lived, and will continue to live, for ever, in the light of his daughters' genius, a light undoubtedly kindled and fanned into flame by his stories often brilliantly recounted: particularly those tales of his father's experiences as a boy on the banks of the Boyne.

Through all the changing scenes of his life he never forgot the old home at Ballynaskeagh.

CHAPTER 18

CANTABRIGIAN COMES HOME

" OH Hugh ! what do you think ! Patrick's comin' home;
he should be here any day now." So said Alice one
day in the autumn of 1816. The postman had just arrived,
and she had an opened letter in her hand. " An' what's more
he's goin'' to preach the sermon at Drumballyroney on
Sunday."

Soon the family were agog with excitement. They were
now in the final and most pretentious of the Brontë homes:
a house with three bedrooms upstairs and two rooms down-
stairs. It was situated beside the McClory home, and directly
opposite the glen which the imaginative family had divided
into three compartments: the Cockpit, the Concert Green,
and the Devil's Dining Room.

The following day a conveyance drew up and there he
was: tall, handsome, and dignified, looking, as his proud
mother thought, every inch a gentleman in his shining clerical
garb. He had now been appointed deacon at Fulham in
London and was shortly to become a fully-fledged priest to
take up a curacy at Wethersfield in Essex.

" Why Patrick it's lovely to see you," said Alice. As she
hugged him to her breast she had difficulty in keeping back
the tears from her eyes. " Come on in," she said, " an' let
me have a good look at you ! Man yer lookin' wonderful !
An' you have a B.A. now an' ye'll soon be the Reverend.
Oh, Patrick, Ah'm so proud of you ! Ah just hope ye won't
find us all too humble for ye."

"Don't talk nonsense, Mama," Patrick replied. "As if I haven't been longing for this moment ever since I went away. You're looking fine yourself, and as lovely as ever. When I was over the hill and saw the Mournes, I felt as if I'd never been away. Cambridge and London are wonderful places, but give me the County Down hills every time. And how's everybody?"

"They're all fine; all workin' hard an' makin' good money. All the boys are at the road makin' now—some new process—Mac . . . Mac. . . ."

"Macadam," Hugh said.

"Aye, that's it; anyhow it's doin' well; an' they're drawin' the stones from our own lan'. We have quite a bit o' lan' now; you know that. Your father's a wonderful man; he's a great head on him."

"Och, sure here he is!" And at that precise moment in walked Hugh, as big as ever, as hearty as ever; but looking his age, Patrick thought.

"Why if it isn't his reverence!" said Hugh, obviously delighted to see his son, but for the moment almost shy of him for they now both lived in such different worlds.

Hugh shook hands, sat down at the table, put his cap on his knees and said: "Aye, aye, sure it's glad Ah am to see ye; Ah heard ye'd done great things at the college over there. What's this ye are? Bachelor o' Arts! Man alive, Ah never thought Ah'd live to see a son o' mine with such an honour!"

"Oh I don't know; it's not such a great honour. There are lots of others with their degrees. I was lucky; I have a good memory; and I suppose I worked hard. You and Mama always taught me the value of hard work; and you gave me every encouragement. Besides, it's only a beginning. Soon I'll be a fully-fledged priest; and then my life's work will really begin."

"An' Ah hear yer goin' to preach for us on Sunday at Drumballyroney. Ye'll have a good congregation all right; the word's gone round; everybody's keen to hear ye," Hugh said with pride in his voice.

As soon as the girls learned that their brother was home they slipped upstairs to tidy up. The younger ones, Alice, aged ten; the twins, Rose and Sara, aged thirteen were, of course, a little shy and slightly fearful of this scholar brother of whom they had heard so much. Mary and Jane, however, being older, threw their arms around him and kissed him, while Patrick for his part looked them over at arm's length and said: " My, how good-looking you all are ! "

And good-looking they were, though strangely enough the only one to marry was Sara, who was to follow in their mother's footsteps by having ten children. Why did they not marry ? Which, in turn, prompts the question: did they have the opportunity ? Possibly not, for, as we said earlier, they appear to have been of the strong handsome type, rather than of the essentially feminine type. It might also be argued that where love binds is the place where people wish to remain.

One by one the men came in from their several jobs: all strong, hearty, and handsome as you make them—and all men now. First there was Billy, a man of the world who had already fought the good fight with the United Irishmen at Ballynahinch. He was often to recount the story of his exploits: he had been recruited at a local barn where he was asked:

" Are you straight ? "
" I am," was the reply.
" How straight ? "
" Straight as a rush."
" What have you got in your hand ? "
" A green bough."
" Where did it first grow ? "
" In America."
" Where did it bud ? "
" In France."
" Where are you going to plant it ? "
" In the Crown of Great Britain."

After some preliminary training he and his friends, both Catholic and Protestant, were to set off with patriotic fervour in their hearts, and whatever firearms were available on their shoulders. After the rout and their dispersal, it was a case of every man for himself; Billy took to the bogs of the Lagan valley; and, circling Dromara, he crossed the Flough Bog to Banbridge, home, and disillusionment. Maybe disillusionment caused him to open a pub on the Knock Hill in which he was the best advertisement for his excellent whiskey, for he could drink more than most. However, as they would have said locally, " he caught himself on "; married, and had six successful sons.

Then there was big-hearted Hugh.

" At arguing, too, the parson owned his skill
    But e'en though vanquished, he could argue still."

One night during the potato failure he tried to poison the devil—who was blamed for the failure—by throwing bad potatoes at him in the Devil's Dining Room. He was never the same man afterwards ! He had the reputation of being fearless, undaunted by man, ghost, devil, or any fiend of earth or hell. He, with his brother, was to become a great builder of roads and player of fiddles.

As for a reviewer who dared to criticise *Jane Eyre* adversely, he treated him with the same scorn as he treated the devil. Armed with a shillelagh he made the journey from Warrenpoint to Liverpool, via Haworth, to London. And what is more, he walked all the way from Liverpool to Haworth on foot ! Charlotte didn't think much of her belligerent Irish uncle's Galahad mission, nor did he think much of Charlotte whom he described as a *poor frachter*—in other words a weak chicken. He expected a great genius to be as great in size as one of his sisters.

Fortunately for both Hugh and the reviewer, the latter, whoever he was, was not at home when the shillelagh-armed Hugh arrived at John Murray's, the publishers. Thus the mission of revenge turned into a sightseeing tour, during which the would-be avenger heard all the sounds, and saw all the sights of London, including a sight of the Queen herself.

Lastly, on that evening there were the gentle shoemaker, James, and the gentlemanly Walsh. James also visited Haworth and spent some time there; on his return he is reported to have said of Charlotte that " she was tarrible sharp and inquisitive." Alice—presumably the young sister— described her brother James as one who " took a hand at everything and was very smart and active with his tongue."

Walsh and Hugh were mates in everything: workmates and music-mates. They built walls together and played the fiddle together; and they both had a penchant for hard liquor. Walsh also established a shebeen; his, however, was down in a cottage in the hamlet, whereas Hugh's was up on the heights of the Knock.

Walsh came to fame when he publicly fought a local bully in a Rathfriland field.

It appears that Walsh's girl complained to him about the treatment of her little crippled brother on the way home from Ballynafern School. The boy was constantly arriving home dirty, covered with mud, and in tears. No Brontë could resist such an appeal. Consequently he waited and watched. He saw the boys remove the child's crutches; and before Walsh could prevent it, they had pushed the terrified cripple into a pond, so that he was up to his neck in water, while they danced around shouting: " Cleshbeg ! Cleshbeg ! Cleshbeg !" Walsh rescued the child; punished the boys; and made them carry the lad home on their backs.

Angry words about the business had already passed between a Mr. Sam Clarke—a relative of the boys concerned—and Walsh; but when the boys, to offset their own disgraceful behaviour, had stated that Walsh had assaulted them, a challenge was issued by Clarke. This was what Walsh had been waiting for; he took up the challenge without further parley.

The upshot of it was that the fight would take place in a hill-surrounded field outside Rathfriland on an arranged day at twelve noon. The news went around like wildfire. On the day spectators flocked to their vantage points; they came from town and townland, from field and farm, meadow and mountain, in every form of transport: horses and horse-carts, traps and side-cars, coaches, buggies, and even donkeys.

It has been stated that the mothers of the two boys fed them like fighting cocks to increase their energy output; this seems scarcely credible. Knowing mothers to be what they are, and in particular knowing Walsh's mother, one would have thought that they would have done all in their power to stop such an adventure. It has also been stated that Sam's mother said to him: " Sam, my son, may you never get bite nor sup from me more, if you do not lick the mongrel." When this got around it swung all the sympathies in Brontë's favour, especially as he was the less favoured man physically.

Whether organized according to Queensberry Rules or not is not known, but there certainly appears to have been organization: a ring, seconds, stewards and all the rest.

Albeit, with their girls in support and their mothers at the ringside, at the drop of a hat the two were at it hammer and tongs. Their bare-handed blows rained at each other for more than three hours in a way that would have made a heavyweight champion quail. In complete silence they battered and slugged and bashed each other until the girls had to cover their eyes to shut out the sight of their bloodied faces.

Then cutting into the silence a voice was heard ringing across the field; it was the voice of Walsh's girl shouting:

" Walsh, my boy, go in and avenge my brother and the mongrel ! "

Walsh heard her; this was just what he needed to stimulate him to the final effort. One more volley of blows; his adversary was on his knees; another and he was flattened, unconscious.

When it was all over, and after Sam had recovered, the two shook hands; they remained friends for the rest of their lives. Walsh, for his part, rarely again referred to this event of which he seemed to be heartily ashamed. Later he was to marry the girl; he had two sons, both of whom ended tragically: one was drowned in the Bann, the other drowned himself in drink.

All these things had happened, or were about to happen, to the members of this singular family of individuals. Doubtless those that had already taken place were talked about when the family found themselves reunited around the fireside on that first September evening of Patrick's return.

After so many years of study, and after so many years when, in a sense, he couldn't be quite himself, to be able to relax here at home for a while was an immense relief. To walk around the farm, to see the cows, pigs, and poultry; to see all the most recently acquired land; to watch and take an interest in the labour on the land without being involved; all this was what he needed to rest his tired brain. But above all to walk along well-loved, leafy lanes, to climb to the cairn-topped summit of the Knock, and to look away across the hummocked hills of the Down valleys to the Mourne foot; this was joy unspeakable, especially at a time when the love of God and all he thought he could do for Him was surging through his whole being.

Of course they made a tremendous fuss of him; the girls in particular could scarcely do enough for him. What would he like for his breakfast, his dinner, his supper? They were getting away a little from the old sowins and fadge days; there were more meat, more bacon, and more eggs. But Patrick would have no special treatment. He had lived frugally all his life; he would go on living frugally until the end of his days.

" No ! no ! no! thank you ! " he would say. " You'll have me completely spoiled. Too much strong food doesn't agree with me anyhow. I'll just have the same as everyone else."

" Anything ye'd like to do to-day, Patrick ? " one of the
boys would say, " Ah could take an hour or two off; bit o'
ridin', shootin' or anything ye'd like; what about it ? "

" Shooting, yes. I used to be a fair hand with the gun,
but I'm a bit out of practice. Did a bit when I was in the
Corps at Cambridge."

" Right ! We'll go off at dawn to-morrow morning;
that's the best time."

And so while September mists still lay in the glen, and
along the river valleys, they were up and away; and Patrick,
who showed himself to be a good shot, enjoyed every minute.
He had that skill in the understanding and use of firearms so
characteristic of his fellow countrymen. For the remainder of
his stay he practised pistol shooting every day; and he became
so competent that he won many local competitions. He took
a hand also at the local bowling game; this consisted in half
bowling, half throwing a heavy metal ball along the road for
miles. One way or another the newly-fledged parson proved
himself to be a good sportsman.

But the family *pièce de résistance* was undoubtedly the evening concert on the Concert Green. As soon as they came in
from the harvest fields out would come the fiddles; and, as
the sun began to scatter its light on the western hill-tops, they
would make one of the most colourful scenes ever to be known
in that autumn coloured country. And of course their highly
coloured homespuns added greatly to the fiesta-like atmosphere
of the performance.

As Hugh and Walsh began to bow their fiddle strings, with
one girl spinning her wheel airily, the remainder of the boys
and girls were soon spinning over the short grass in a beautifully rhythmic pattern of dances: jigs, reels, hornpipes, and
all the rest were danced with almost professional decorum and
discipline. Then as the last lingering light painted the
westerly hills, each boy would bow to one of the girls with
as much cavalier grace as one would expect to find in the most
sophisticated ballroom. Though Patrick took no part in the

Glasgar Manse—where "Jane Eyre" was read—possibly for the first time.

Drumballyroney Church and School.

dancing, he watched with interest this fascinating family festival.

Came Sunday, and Patrick's first sermon. Soon the car was ready, with the horse standing patiently while the girls put the last touches to their ribboned hair, and the boys, still not unconscious of their appearance, tightened their ties and combed their hair into place behind their caps.

Patrick, who had been up since dawn and had been quietly walking the wild woods, alternately going over his sermon and praying, was awarded the place of honour, while old Hugh and Alice sat proudly beside him. " Gee up ! " and they were off under interlacing trees already shot with early autumn's flaming colours. How happy they were, Patrick thought, as they bowled along; how much happier he would be on the return journey !

Soon they were high up at the hill-placed church of Drumballyroney. They felt like, as indeed they *were* on this occasion, very important persons. On arrival someone came forward to hold the horse's head, while others assisted Alice and Hugh and the girls to ground level. In a moment they were shaking hands with friends all around, Patrick in the meantime having disappeared with the welcoming rector with whom he went into the vestry to don his vestments.

During the opening hymns, prayers and liturgies, the heart of one woman at least thumped, as *she* thought, almost audibly. But she needn't have worried for when Patrick entered the pulpit and began to speak he was in complete command; and he then began a habit which he held to for the remainder of his professional life: he used neither script nor notes. Indeed his youngest sister, Alice, told a gentleman whom the author of this account knew, that ". . . . he preached a gran' sermon and never had anything in his han' the whole time."

There is no record of what he said, though it has been suggested that his text may have been that used as the theme of a poem written at this time;

" Study to shew thyself approved unto God, a workman that needeth not be ashamed, rightly dividing the word of truth " (2 Tim. 2: 15). If so it was certainly well-chosen for this congregation of village craftsmen, and peasant country-men. And they were impressed, not merely because here was a local boy made good, but also because of his palpable sincerity and fine delivery.

After the final hand-shakings and congratulations in which Alice and Hugh were to share, they were all soon on the happy road for home, their horse prancing proudly as though he too sensed the joy of the occasion. And then there was the very special Sunday dinner—always special in the country—but more special than ever on this occasion. You may be sure, also, that for once Patrick let himself go, and did full justice to the chicken and ham, and the egg-flavoured and coloured rice pudding that followed.

But it all had to end; Patrick had to go. He didn't know, nor did Alice and Hugh know, that they would never see him again. Nor was Alice aware of the fact that in two years' time she would be saying her final farewell to Hugh and happiness. That she was to have the most of her large family around her for the next fourteen years was a comfort, but not a compensation.

All aboard ! A last hand-clasp from Hugh, a last hug from Alice, and Patrick's ship was on its way from Warrenpoint, down Carlingford, to the sea. As he looked upwards at the silent hills above the silent sea, Patrick's thoughts were on the strange story of his father's early life beyond those hills; he decided that he must store this in his memory so that he could pass it on to his own children, if he were lucky enough to have any children.

He wondered what life would have in store for him. Though he had high hopes, he was thoughtful enough, and he had read and seen enough of life, to enable him to realize that it wasn't all going to be a bed of roses; that unseen dangers, difficulties, twists and temptations must lie ahead; but he felt strong and resourceful; and he had that powerful faith that made him realize that come what may, he could go out into the world with his hand in the hand of God.

And he needed all his faith. In a few years' time—in about six years—he was to marry his Cornish Methodist, Mary Branwell, who probably already carried within her the seeds of the disease that was to be the cause of most of the tragedies of his life. In a few years' time he was to be settled in the Yorkshire village of Haworth, on its bleak height, with the bleak, lonely moors rolling onwards for ever, as it seemed, into the distance. Here first Mary, or Maria, his wife, after nine years, was to go; then in succession, year by year—sometimes month by month—a melancholy procession was to be seen passing from the house to the church, and from the church to the graveyard in sight of the house: young Maria, Elizabeth, Bramwell, Emily, Anne buried in Scarborough, Charlotte, until finally Patrick was left alone. Would it have been any wonder if he had cursed the God who had bowed his head under such a weight of sorrow? Would it have been any wonder if, in his moments of loneliness, the thought had crossed his mind that the happiest time of his life had been spent among the hills and dales of Emdale, Lisnacreevy and Ballynaskeagh in the County Down?

The thought must have occurred to him that God moves in a mysterious way; and, had he been able to look ahead over a century or so, he would have seen that the brief mortality of his family was to be translated into heights of immortality greater than those of any other family in the whole history of English literature.

In the meantime what was happening at Ballynaskeagh? We already know about some of the most exciting and interesting events. Before the Haworth people had begun to make literary history, three of the older generation had already been buried at Drumballyroney: Hugh, whom we first met by the Boyne Water, and his wife, Alice; and the first daughter, Sara. But the remainder of the family was still intact, and working out their destinies in their united—and sometimes different—ways: farming, road building, pub-

making and shoe-making. One does not know to what extent they were readers; but evidently they could read with some discrimination.

One day there was considerable excitement when Hugh arrived in with a parcel from Haworth. " What the hell ! " said Hugh, " three books if ye plase. No, one book in three volumes; what's this ? *Jane Eyre* by Carver Bell. Now who would that be ? "

At this point one of the quicker minded women joined in: " *Carver Bell*—C.B.—och, of course: Charlotte Brontë ! Man you're slow Hugh, it's a book by Charlotte."

" Holy smokes ! " Hugh exclaimed, " so it is; but why the hell didn't she write it under her own name; she must have had sumpin' to hide ! "

" Let's have a look at it," they all said in chorus, but try as they would, they couldn't make head nor tail of it. It was quite unlike any book they had seen before.

" A lot o' oul' nonsense ! " one of the men said. " That's what comes o' livin' among all them foreigners in Englan'."

" Tell ye what," one of the girls said. " Take it across to the Rev. McKee an' ask him what he thinks about it."

" Dammit, the very thing ! " Hugh replied. " Ah'll do that straight away."

Accordingly Hugh wrapped up the books in a red hand-kerchief and hurried down the road to The Manse, where he was ushered into a room in which Mr. McKee was just about to have his tea.

" Well, what's the trouble now, Hughie ? "

" It's just about these, sir, they've just arrived from the niece Charlotte. We were just wonderin' . . . mebbe ye'd have a look at them, 'cause we were a bit doubtful. Ye see she doesn't even use her own name. You bein' a Minister o' God, an' a scholar, would know if they were all right."

" Of course, of course, Hughie ! Now let's see. Oh, by the way, help yourself to tea ! "

While Hugh indulged himself with an excellent tea, Mr. McKee, forgetting all about *his,* addressed himself to the books. And he read on, and on, and on, sometimes frowning, sometimes laughing and occasionally gesticulating. " Wonderful ! Wonderful ! " Such exclamations would escape his lips now and then. At last, when Hugh had almost given up hope of getting home that evening, he suddenly jumped from the chair in which he was reading and said excitedly:

" Hughie, the book bears the Brontë stamp in every sentence and idea, and it is the grandest novel that has been produced in my time." And then he added: " The child, Jane Eyre, is your father in petticoats, and Mrs. Reed is the wicked uncle by the Boyne."

Having thanked Mr. McKee, Hugh went home in a state of elation. " Well," the family said, as soon as he arrived, " what did he say ? "

" What did he say ? Well Ah'll tell yez. He said the book was just gran', an' one of the greatest novels he had ever read."

Which leaves us with little more to say, except that the family was to go on in the district up to the present day when one still sees vans bearing the inscription "Brontë Bros, Contractors." One would like to end on this happy note, but regretful as it may be, life rarely ends happily as the following two letters illustrate; at the same time they give us a further insight into the character of the man Patrick Brontë.

Haworth,
Near Keighley,
December 2nd, 1858.

Dear Brother,

I hope that you are now in better health than formerly. My sister Mary's letter gave me to understand that you were in but a very delicate state of health. I should think that if you cannot manage the farming business my brother James would be able to supply your place. From the newspapers I learn that farmers in Ireland are now doing very well, and if they would in Ireland leave off their Bible warning, murdering, and quarrelling with each other, and as rational beings attend to the improvement of their country, owing to its good soil and harbours, mines and many other peculiar advantages, Ireland, instead of being a degraded country, would be one of the most respectable portions of the globe. Trade here has for a very long time been very flat, but it is now something better; nevertheless vast numbers are now out of work, and owing to this and the high price of provisions, there is a great deal of distress, and the poor rates are high, but we hope for better times. God is over all, and the supreme disposer of all events, and He will have mercy on the poor, and send relief in the best time and manner. Considering my advanced age, I have much reason to be thankful to God that I am yet able to preach once or twice on Sundays, and to do some duty besides. My son-in-law still continues to be with me and is very kind. He generally sees your letters. Hoping you are all well and doing well in reference to time and eternity.

I remain,
Your affectionate brother,
P. Brontë.

To Mr. H. Brontë, Ballina, near Loughbrickland, Ireland.
                              Haworth,
                                      Near Keighley,
                                              February 1st, 1859.

Dear Sister,

I am sorry to learn that my sister Sara is unwell. May God for Christ's sake comfort and support her, and save her with an everlasting salvation. I have herewith sent her £1 in a post office order. It is a small sum but it will provide for her some medicine and will be useful in other ways. You must go to the Post Office in Loughbrickland and sign the order, and get the money in your own name. The boyish papers you sent me remind me of old times. David Cruickshanks, which you mention, must now be an old man. I remember him well. Most of those whom I once knew must now be dead, and Ireland must, in many respects, be greatly changed from what it was when I resided in it. I am, through divine mercy, as well as can be reasonably expected at my advanced age of more than eighty-one years. I still preach once on Sunday, and Mr. Nicholls, who is very obliging and willing, preaches twice. We have still a great many calls from lords and ladies and others, but they do not stop long, as I cannot do with much company. The day is very dark and my sight is very dim, so you will have some difficulty in reading this letter. I am glad to know that all my brothers and sisters except one are well.

                    Your affectionate brother,
                          P. Brontë.

Miss Mary Brontë, near Loughbrickland.

And just one fina comment before we close the story of this remarkable family. Many books, controversial, critical, patronizing, and complimentary, have been written about those people, but through all this literary wealth, a novel fact has emerged in recent years: the giant at the centre of much of this immense outpouring of words has become the Rev. Patrick Brontë of Ballynaskeagh. That a father should have become at least as immortal as his immortal daughters must be something unique in the annals of literature.

Though sunshine and snow, summer and winter, seed-time and harvest, have come and gone throughout two hundred years since that fateful night, 17th March, 1777, Emdale, Ballynaskeagh, Drumballyroney, and all the lands and townlands round about remain much as they were; but through two famous books—*Jane Eyre* and *Wuthering Heights*—these places have become for ever indissolubly joined to Haworth in Yorkshire.

Rostrevor, Co. Down.
February 24th, 1778.